I0517846

The Leadership Playbook for the Trades

GET SHIT DONE!

How to Build a Strong Team, a Profitable Business, and a Lasting Legacy

NATE AGENTIS

LESSONS OF HOPE FROM A 3RD-GEN PLUMBER

Get Shit Done!

How to Build a Strong Team, a Profitable Business, and a Lasting Legacy

Copyright © 2025. Nate Agentis. All rights reserved. No part of this book may be reproduced by any mechanical, photographic, or electronic process, or in the form of a phonographic recording; nor may it be stored in a retrieval system, transmitted, or otherwise be copied for public or private use—other than for "fair use" as brief quotations embodied in articles and reviews—without prior written permission of the publisher.

This publication is designed to provide accurate and authoritative information regarding the subject matter covered. It is sold with the understanding that the publisher is not engaged in rendering legal, accounting, or other professional services. If you require legal advice or other expert assistance, you should seek the services of a competent professional.

Design and cover art by Peaceful Profits.

Disclaimer: The author makes no guarantees to the results you'll achieve by reading this book. All business requires risk and hard work. The results and client case studies presented in this book represent results achieved working directly with the author. Your results may vary when undertaking any new business venture or marketing strategy.

To my loving wife and best friend,

You have been with me through every mountaintop and valley—through
the highs and lows of life and business. Your unwavering, ferocious love
for God and our family has been my anchor, helping me heal from the
past, stay on track, and pursue dreams bigger than we ever imagined.
Your strength and devotion inspire me daily, and I am forever grateful for
the life we are building together.

To my kids,

Your constant encouragement inspires me to be better every day. You are
living healthier, Godlier, and smarter than I ever did, and watching you
grow fills me with great joy and hope for the future.

And to my dad,

Your sacrifices, hard work, and vision paved the way for everything I've
been blessed to build. You created something from nothing, and your
faith, passion for plumbing, and dedication to providing for our family
have produced a harvest that will last for generations. I am forever in awe
of your legacy and grateful to carry it forward.

CONTENTS

YOU'RE THE HERO
IN THIS STORY

As a tech in the trades, you're probably neck-deep in hard work, and you may not feel like much of a hero right now. I can relate. The work we do is often undervalued by our culture to the point that we're overshadowed by big executive jobs, Wall Street gurus, IT gigs that pay $80k straight out of school, and even YouTube influencer sensations—but we're not the second-class service providers we're often made out to be.

In fact, I'll go so far as to say we ARE heroes!

Our entire career is stepping into people's messes and emergency situations to restore peace to their lives. You and I both know what happens when big execs, Wall Street gurus, and YouTubers have a pipe burst. In that moment, their catastrophe becomes our call, and because it's what we do, we get right to it. But if we don't have our businesses organized in a way that flows, we end up giving up our own peace of mind while we work hard to restore peace for others.

The reason I wrote this book is that, as a third-generation plumber and business owner, I've learned a thing or two about a better way to serve clients that also serves you.

To give you an overview, there are three main points I want you to get from reading this book.

1. As someone in the trades, you're not a second-class service provider and you don't have to sacrifice your own peace in the process of serving your clients.

2. Humility is key, and accountability is what keeps you on track. You must accept the need for change in your business and set up the right systems for honest feedback. When you have both, you'll be able to grow and scale your business in a way that supports you.

3. To scale your business effectively and sustainably, you need to grow strategically, and at the right pace, in the five key areas of the Leadership Playbook for the Trades (I'll share more on this with you in Part 2). This helps you maintain balance while seeing steady progress and growth.

Listen, I know you've constantly got your nose to the grindstone. What you do is important because you're not just fixing pipes or wiring; you're solving problems and bringing a critical sense of peace and security to the homes of your clients. If you're going to grow your business (and keep your peace of mind while you do it), then a few things are going to have to change. I know you're not surprised to hear that. It's likely why you picked up this book in the first place.

With that in mind, my highest hope for you is this...

I want you to find the courage to stop doing things the way they've always been done and start building a legacy that improves the lives of your family, your customers, and your community.

I know change isn't easy. It takes a lot of small steps to get there. There's really no secret sauce or anything magical that's going to happen. I'm not here trying to be a genius. You probably already know a lot of the right things to do; sometimes you just can't see how to do them clearly.

So, what should you expect as you read this book?

First, I'm going to talk about the importance of growing and scaling your business the right way so that you can handle any change or crisis. We'll take a look at examples and stories and delve into where you currently are in your business. In the process, I'll share how I came to discover this solution.

In Part 2, we'll look more at the five pillars of the Leadership Playbook for the Trades; Healthy Owner, Sticky Culture, Skilled Technicians, Efficient Operations, and Clear Metrics. And, in Part 3, I'll give you some practical steps to get you started so you can begin to create the success you're looking for.

You may love being in the field. But, as you transition to being an owner and leader, you have to start thinking strategically and setting goals for the business, your team, and yourself. To make sure you get all the tools you need to make the transition, I've packed this book full of practical applications that are meant to be building blocks to create a solid foundation. Follow the steps and you'll find yourself running a business in a way that perhaps you never thought was possible. I'm not just talking about revenue goals; I'm talking about freedom, legacy, and resilience. So, if you are looking to transition from just being in a truck and using your hands, to learning what it takes to grow and scale a business, then you will find what you need in this book.

My Goal for You

I want you to start implementing healthy changes in your life and business before you even finish reading this book. Going through tools from the Leadership Playbook for the Trades, you will see what healthy looks like and recognize what changes need to be made.

Maybe you feel like you've been struggling for years yet your business and life are not at the level you thought they would be. You're burning out, and maybe you don't even know it yet. I want to help you see the value in what truly matters and start making changes now BEFORE you burn out or burn it all to the ground.

Reasons for This Book

I wrote this book because I believe it's my God-given calling. I stayed in plumbing, even during times when I hated it and wanted out. I overcame many seasons of change, crisis, and setbacks in my life—loss, financial stress, tears, and burnout. But after facing all the chaos, I realized that I was put here to share stories and wisdom with others. Once I accepted this calling, things shifted and that's when I went from a guy who'd inherited a business he thought he didn't want, to recognizing what I had, and my company, Hope for the Trades, was born.

This book is here to help you, as someone in the trades, learn from my wins, breaks, and mistakes. Not just mine, but others who have been there and done that too. I want to help owners and managers move successfully from a truck into a true leadership role. I also want to save you from sacrificing too much of yourself as you grow your business, because that's when good people burn out, quit, or go back to being in a truck. Taking the step from doing the work to leading the work requires a different mindset, different processes, and a different approach. Most people fail to make the transition because they just don't know the right steps to take as a leader.

I want you to understand that you'll still work hard, but you'll also take a vacation, exercise, spend time with your kids, and pour that same hard work into your marriage.

Let me ask you this...

How many people in the trades do you know (counting yourself if that's applicable) who have sacrificed everything but still don't have a solid retirement? Are you still paying off a mortgage? Has all the work you've done gotten you anywhere?

When I started taking small steps to find that balance for me, people started asking questions and wanting to know more, and the snowball just kept growing. I don't feel like I have "arrived" and I definitely still make mistakes, but I feel like this book can help get you on the right path, too.

You'll need to have faith. You've got to believe. My faith in God helped me know that I could ride the storms. I didn't really know the outcome, but I knew that if I kept working at doing the right things, even when it was hard or when no one else was looking, there would be some kind of blessing on the other side.

You Don't Have to Do It Alone

I've had good friends and coworkers come alongside me and help me grind it out to make the changes I needed to move toward my vision and bring the organization forward. It took humility and outside wisdom to see better perspectives. That's how we got to where we are...together.

In many ways, the trades get learning right. Apprenticeships are quite common and we all become proficient in our trade from the ground up. As technicians, we're better for it. But when it comes to growing a trade *business*, there isn't enough mentorship around. Our needs are different from other businesses. Our hiring, supplies, customers, and processes are different. General "how to" books on business growth give us only part of what we need. My hope is that this book can fill the gap.

Take a moment to imagine the impact you can have if you grow a business that you can scale well. Imagine the impact on your technicians, your office, the families you serve, your marriage, and the communities you work in. When you get this right, your success will be like compound interest on an investment. It will keep on growing. That's the kind of impact a hero can have.

You're not alone. Your problems are things that many of us face. I challenge you to slow down and recognize that it's okay to get help and seek wisdom. I want to help you be the hero of your story.

Read this book, do the assessments, and start fighting and working hard for the right things. If you need help, give us a call. We'd love to come alongside you! so you can get shit done…in the *right* way!

Nate Agentis

Hope for the Trades

PART 1
You're Not Alone

CHAPTER 1

TEARS IN THE TRADES

Like you, I'm a tradesman but I don't generally feel like a hero. When I started working in our family's plumbing company as a kid, I certainly had no idea what it took to be a business owner. Learning what it takes to run a company well hasn't been easy. In fact, it started with a lot of tears.

In February 2012, my mom got sick, and by December, she was gone. Those ten months were some of the hardest I've ever faced. My parents, who had always been the guiding force behind our plumbing business, walked away after her diagnosis, and in an instant, I was in charge.

Everything shifted and I wasn't ready.

There I was with three kids at home, an adoption process underway, and my wife doing everything she could to hold it all together. Life was already full, but now the business was squarely on my shoulders. I went from being a guy in the trenches to being the one responsible for keeping the whole thing from falling apart.

Those first months were pure survival mode. I woke up every day, reacting to whatever crisis hit first. The people I had been working alongside for years—people who were once my coworkers and even friends—were now looking to me for leadership. But I had no idea what I was doing. The whole business was a mess: no systems, no clear communication, nothing. Yet somehow, we were growing.

But growing just made everything worse. The more we grew, the more chaotic it all became. We needed a new way forward, a foundation that could support *growth* instead of just survival.

First Successes: Creating Clarity from Chaos

The turning point came when we started defining roles. We mapped out every job and clearly defined each person's role. No more guessing. No more wondering who was responsible for what.

It was slow, but within a year or two, things began to stabilize. The chaos that had marked those early months started to fade. By early 2017, we weren't just surviving; we were building something solid. As we built systems that could support growth, we upgraded our customer relationship management system (CRM), redefined communication processes, and put key players in the right roles. For the first time, we had structure.

Not everyone was on board with the new structure, or the accountability that came with it. Employees were used to the old way of doing things and some of them resisted the changes. In fact, some of the hardest parts of this transition were dealing with people who couldn't handle the changes. Some ended up leaving the company and, honestly, that was tough. For those who stayed, the transformation was real.

Suddenly, it wasn't just me trying to hold everything together. The team began to step up. They knew what their responsibilities were, and they started to own them. We didn't just react to problems anymore. We thought ahead and planned for growth.

It wasn't easy, but we stuck with it, and gradually, the chaos faded. Instead of feeling like we were hanging on by a thread, we were moving forward with purpose.

I want that feeling of purpose for you as well. As you start to implement the Leadership Playbook for the Trades, expect some clogs along the way. You will likely get resistance. But, you'll ultimately find that people really appreciate knowing what's expected of them.

Living in the New World

Today, the business feels like a different place. It's no longer in the midst of chaos. We have systems in place that allow the company to operate smoothly and it runs like a well-oiled machine.

Everyone knows their role, their responsibilities, and what success looks like. Meetings are productive and focused on driving the business forward. Processes are in place to ensure that every task is completed efficiently and there's accountability at every level. It's not just about business growth. It's about having peace of mind knowing that standard procedures are in place and important metrics are being tracked so the business can run without me. You can experience this difference and have that kind of peace in your business too. Since we implemented the Leadership Playbook for the Trades, the difference has been night and day. Here are just some of the positive changes we've seen.

- *Decreased employee turnover.* People aren't leaving because they feel lost or unsupported. People stay because they know what's expected of them, feel more secure, see career paths available for them to grow, and feel part of something bigger.

- *Revenue growth.* By defining roles, refining processes, and improving communication, we've been able to scale our operations and take on more clients, all while delivering a higher level of service. Our customers know what to expect, and our team knows how to deliver. Our systems allow us to focus on the right opportunities, so we're not chasing after

11

every little thing anymore. We became strategic, and that focus led to steady revenue growth.

- *Operational efficiency.* We're leaner and more efficient than ever. Gone is the chaos that defined our days in the past. Now, the systems and processes keep things running smoothly. We know who's responsible for what, and when something goes wrong, we know exactly where to look to find or create the solution.

- *Peace of mind.* I no longer wake up every day with anxiety wondering what's going to go wrong next. I can be present for my family, emotionally as well as physically, instead of being constantly consumed by the business. That's a real, measurable difference in my life.

Creating and implementing the Leadership Playbook for the Trades has changed everything for me. I'm not tied to the day-to-day grind anymore. I get to focus on the bigger picture, on growth and innovation, and on spending time with my family. I have coffee with my wife every morning. I work out regularly. I take vacations. I can have dinner with my kids and not worry that something's falling apart back at work. Instead, I get to lead, think strategically, and plan for the future. The systems we built didn't just save the business. They gave me back my life.

What would change for you if you weren't so consumed by your business? What big ideas could you bring in if you had the time and energy to focus on the bigger picture? How would your personal life and your relationships benefit from being able to be more present?

I'm not the only one who's benefited from this approach. There have been profound effects on people inside our company, as well as in other companies. The following are just a few examples.

Case Study 1: Brian's Evolution

Brian has been with our company for over 30 years. He was one of my dad's earliest hires—a tough, no-nonsense guy who came out of the military and went straight into the plumbing trenches. Back then, Brian wasn't exactly management material. He was definitely "rough" around the edges and didn't love working with people. As the owner's kid, I'd often be the target of his and others' razzing. Brian was the kind of guy you could count on to always get the job done, plain and simple, but he wasn't the one you wanted in front of clients or mentoring newcomers.

As the company changed, over time, I saw a shift in Brian. He was capable and skilled, and I saw the potential for him to step up. Despite the sarcasm and rough edges, he showed leadership skills and an ability to run a project. So, we worked with him, coached him on leadership, and transitioned him into a management role.

After years of dedication, through our commitment to him and his commitment to growth, Brian has now been with the company for 32 years and serves as our Chief Service Operator. He oversees 40 plumbers and handles everything from hiring and firing to strategy meetings, growth planning, and technician training.

With the right systems in place and the patience to grow at a steady pace, Brian has been able to thrive. These structures made his path clear and allowed him to transition from the guy who just wanted to fix things to the one driving the business forward.

Case Study 2: Matt's Transformation

Matt found me at a conference and was in the same place I'd been—stuck—feeling like he was just treading water. He and his wife were running their plumbing business much like ours started—grinding it out and trying to do everything themselves. They handled every task, answered phones, and took every service call. It was exhausting, and they couldn't figure out how to grow without working themselves to death.

Matt's business was making some money and paying the immediate bills, but it felt chaotic. He said if it grew any more, the demand would overwhelm them, and he and his wife would be ready to throw in the towel. They wanted to grow but had no idea how to break free from the grind.

We got to work implementing the Leadership Playbook for the Trades and the transformation was incredible. In addition to building systems, we defined roles and responsibilities within their business. They hired a team and started putting the processes in place. Within a year, Matt turned his business around. It's not a multi-million-dollar empire yet. Let's be real, trade businesses need to grow at steady, scalable rates. But that's the trajectory he's on. Every year, his business will grow by 30% or more and will be supported by systems that can handle the growth.

My favorite part of Matt's story isn't just that their revenue grew by 38% in 10 months; it's that he and his wife reclaimed their lives. Today, Matt's business is thriving. They've hired employees, divided and conquered their roles, and implemented new systems and processes. They now have more time with their family, less stress on themselves, and a team that knows exactly what they're doing. This kind of business allows them to breathe again.

Case Study 3: Sandy and Ron's Big Shift

Sandy and Ron had been in business for over a decade when they found me. They also were a husband-and-wife team, and like many small business owners, they felt overworked and overwhelmed. They dreamed of growing the business, but also wanted an exit plan. They hoped to sell in five years. The problem was that they didn't have the structure or systems in place to make that a reality. They couldn't grow, and they couldn't exit because everything rested on their shoulders.

So, we got to work. We focused on clarity—defining roles, streamlining communication, and setting up responsibilities at every level. We then broke his and his wife's mish-mashed responsibilities into distinct CEO and COO roles. Once that was in place, we created a strategic one-, three-, and five-year plan with specific goals for their team and set up regular meetings to keep things on track.

As a result, they've experienced real growth and have seen employees step up into leadership roles in ways they never imagined. They even managed to take three weeks off in a row, and the business didn't miss a beat.

With this newfound freedom and success, Sandy and Ron have shifted their five-year exit plan to selling within the next 12 months. They've built something valuable, not just a profitable business, but one with real structure and real appeal for potential buyers.

Case Study 4: Gary Came Back

If you've been in business long enough, you know you'll lose good people along the way. But as I've learned, if they come back, it means you've built something unique.

Years ago, when we increased accountability, it came at a cost. Gary wasn't sure he was ready for that kind of change. He explored other options and landed an opportunity at a competitor where he could make a little extra money. Despite several attempts to get him to stay, Gary decided to leave. He thought the grass would be greener—less pressure and better pay.

But, within a couple of years, he realized what we had built was something special. The systems, the structure, the clarity—it wasn't something he could find anywhere else. Gary discovered that it was the structure we had that helped him do his job better, plus it helped him see what his future career could look like. The chaos of working in an environment without systems simply wasn't worth the extra few bucks an hour.

So, Gary came back to us and is more committed than ever. Now, he understands the value of having rules and systems to create healthy accountability and clarity at every level of the company.

Once you've worked in an environment where everything runs smoothly, you don't want to go back to the chaos. At one point, we had five employees leave for what they thought were better opportunities only to return. They saw that what we'd built was different and worth more than the "shiny-object syndrome" of the short-term opportunities they found elsewhere.

Recap

What ties these success stories together is that you need a solid foundation before you can grow. You can't just keep hustling and hope things work out. What the Leadership Playbook for the Trades offers is more than just a system to boost your revenue or a new software to purchase. It's a blueprint to create a business that works for you, not the other way around.

If you want these kinds of results, commit to the process and do the exercises in this book. These tools are here to guide you and save you from the added tears. This isn't just theory; it's a proven path to building a business that not only survives but thrives.

CHAPTER 2

CHANGE IS NECESSARY

As the old adage goes, "shit happens," and it's the same for change. Change happens, and there's no stopping it whether you're ready for it or not.

As you know, change hit me like a freight train. I was thrust into a leadership role, not because I was ready, but because there was no one else. And the truth was, our business wasn't ready either. It was built entirely around my parents—everything from the way jobs were scheduled to how the phones were answered depended on them. Very quickly, it became painfully clear that I had to make some hard changes if we were going to survive them leaving the business.

Facing Reality—We Weren't Ready for Change

The hardest part of that transition was accepting how unprepared we were. Our business, like so many others, wasn't designed to adapt. We were great at what we did—plumbing—but we weren't great at building a business, and there's a huge difference between the two. The moment I became the boss, all of our cracks started to show. I tried to keep everything the same, to operate the way my parents had, but it just wasn't sustainable.

How about you, would your business be prepared for a big change? Most businesses aren't ready when shifts need to happen. According to the U.S. Bureau of Labor Statistics, approximately

20% of new businesses fail in the first two years and only 25% remain open after year 15. A common reason for their failure is they aren't prepared. Emergencies occur, people leave, and economies shift. Change *will* happen, whether it's something personal like losing a loved one, or something external like a shift in the market. Are you building a business that can adapt and grow through those changes? Or are you just hanging on, hoping things don't fall apart?

In the trades, we're used to fixing things—pipes burst, fixtures fail, systems go wrong—and we're there to get them working again. But running a business? You can't just pull out a wrench and fix that. It's hard to describe the pressure that being an owner puts on you. Maybe you picked up this book because that's exactly how you're feeling. You've got a business to run, people rely on you, and you don't have the luxury of falling apart. I'm glad you're here.

I had to learn the hard way. I was overwhelmed, unsure, and constantly stressed out. I wasn't just dealing with grief. I was trying to save a business on the verge of growing to a size and weight that would crush the systems that supported it—and my back—in the process.

But I felt like I was too BUSY to do anything else!

Busyness Is NOT a Badge of Honor

I know what it feels like to wake up every day with a never-ending list of things to do. I was convinced that if I just worked harder, did more, kept busy, and pushed through, then everything would eventually get better. But, the harder I pushed, the worse it got. I wasn't eating, I wasn't sleeping, and I wasn't present with my family. I became a version of myself that I didn't even recognize. Busyness was my comfort zone, my identity. Slowing down felt like losing.

I was exhausted, spinning my wheels, and never taking a second to step back to reflect on the wins we had, the blessings I had at home, or the things I'd worked months to achieve. The busyness felt validating but it wasn't getting me anywhere. I was burning out fast. My schedule and head were full, but my heart was empty. That's not sustainable, and it's not success.

The truth is, busyness is a trap. People often mistake activity for productivity, but being busy doesn't mean being productive. It's the illusion of progress. It may feel like a cultural badge of honor, but when work becomes your sole identity, it starts to feel like you're never doing enough. The only result is you sacrifice more than you ever intended—your health, your relationships, your joy—just to keep up with the pace you've set for yourself.

If you feel that same frantic, never-ending drive to always be doing something—to keep moving, keep pushing, keep fixing— this book is for you. If you're tired of your answer to "How's it going?" always being "Busy," and your whole identity is wrapped up in work, I get it. You probably believe that's just how life is supposed to be: that's the life of a business owner. But that's a lie and it's costing you more than you signed up for. You're missing the big picture and you may not even know it.

The Turning Point

The turning point came for me when I realized that if I didn't make a change, both the business and my family would suffer. I had to stop doing everything myself. We had to stop operating like a family-owned mom-and-pop shop, overly dependent on one or two people. We had to start thinking like a real business.

That's when I brought in my business partner, Luke. He had a background in corporate America and I needed that kind of structure. We started breaking down the business, job by job and task by task, laying it all out. We redefined every role, laid out a vision, and began to build some much-needed systems. For the first time, we had a plan, an organizational chart, and clarity about who was responsible for what.

We created systems for every task—from how we scheduled jobs to how we communicated with customers. And once those systems were in place, the business began to run more smoothly. I wasn't constantly reacting to fires and drowning in busyness.

For the first time in a long time, I could breathe.

It wasn't an overnight fix, but bit by bit, we started to rebuild. We stopped operating in survival mode and started laying down a foundation that could support the kind of growth we wanted.

Change wasn't just necessary for the business. I, myself, had to change too, in how I approached leadership, how I ran the company, and how I dealt with people. I want you to understand that if your business can't survive without you being constantly busy holding it up, you will burn out. This isn't about doing more. It's about doing things *differently*.

It took a crisis to see that what was needed wasn't more work—it was clarity, structure, and focus. It wasn't easy, and it wasn't quick, but once we made those changes, everything started to click.

The Results: What I Have Now

As a result of making these changes, I have found peace of mind. The business operates smoothly without me needing to be involved in every decision. I have a team I can trust, and they know their roles and responsibilities. The systems we've built allow us to scale and grow without losing control.

I have balance in my life outside of the business, too. I can be present for my family in ways I never could before. I can take a vacation without worrying that everything will fall apart while I'm gone. I've reclaimed my time, and that's priceless.

Before we continue into the rest of the book, let's take a look at the results you are currently getting and where you may need to make some changes.

Self-Assessment: Are You Running Your Business, or Is Your Business Running You?

If you're feeling overwhelmed, stuck in the grind of just being "busy," or unsure how to make meaningful progress, you're not alone. This self-assessment will help you identify the gaps in your business and leadership and show you how the solutions in this book can help you build a thriving, sustainable business that works for you—not the other way around.

In the questions below, rate yourself on a scale from 0 to 5 with 0 meaning "not accurate at all" and 5 meaning "most accurate."

Once you've rated yourself for each statement, total up your scores and then use the Answer Key to determine your next steps.

Success Check-in Statement	Self-Rating
My business has clearly defined roles and responsibilities for each and every team member.	
There are systems in place in my business that allow us to handle tasks and challenges proactively instead of reactively.	
I am confident that my business would function smoothly without me for an extended period of time if I had to or chose to step away.	
I am willing to make difficult decisions and embrace change, even when it's uncomfortable.	
When I'm not sure what decision to make, I seek outside wisdom on the topic.	

I've defined the right things to work on and don't just do the next thing that grabs my attention.	
My daily schedule allows time for strategic planning, not just being busy putting out fires.	
I am able to step back, reflect, and celebrate wins without feeling guilty or like I should move past them quickly.	
My work doesn't consume me to the point where I lose focus on my personal priorities and relationships.	
I regularly invest in systems, tools, and/or coaching and see them as necessary steps for growth.	
I can make spending decisions guided by long-term strategy, not just short-term savings or survival.	
I understand that prioritizing foundational improvements will save time and money in the long run.	
I don't equate being busy with being productive; I know the difference.	
I regularly receive feedback to assess whether the work I'm doing is helping me accomplish my strategic plan.	
I have broken free from the cycle of constant busyness and feel in control of my time and priorities.	
TOTAL UP YOUR SCORE:	

What Your Score Really Means

Score: 0 - 25
Stuck in Survival Mode

Your business is running *you* instead of the other way around. I'd bet you are feeling overwhelmed, reactive, and stuck in a cycle of busyness without making meaningful progress. You probably feel like your to-do list is longer than the hours in the day: you are just trying to stay ahead of the next fire. This book will help you break free from the firefighting by showing you how to create systems, define roles, and build clarity. It will start with you being ready for the change to begin rebuilding your business from the ground up. The Healthy Owner exercises in Part 3 will help you start.

Score: 26 - 50
Caught in the Grind

You're still working hard, but not necessarily working on the right things. You may have some systems in place, but there's still too much of the business that relies on you as the owner. It's likely that your employees are still coming to you with questions about the business that they should be able to handle on their own. By applying the structures of the Leadership Playbook for the Trades (discussed in Part 2), you'll learn how to step back, delegate effectively, and become a more confident leader. You'll find the strategies that will weave into every part of your business to help you get to the right things to work on as the leader of your organization.

Score: 51 - 75
Ready to Thrive

Well done! Your business shows promise and this book will help you refine your systems, delegate more efficiently, and create space for strategic thinking. Get ready to embrace the next-level tools for sustainable growth and improved leadership. The Leadership Playbook for the Trades will also allow you to understand more advanced strategies to solidify your progress.

Recap

Change happens—sometimes slowly and sometimes all at once. The important question is whether or not your business is built in such a way that it would be able to handle it. Most businesses aren't prepared for any kind of change, mine certainly wasn't built to handle the loss of my parents. We kept doing the plumbing work, but the business structures were failing even as we did.

Working harder wasn't fixing the real, foundational problems, it was only burning me out. Being busy and trying to do everything yourself is not a sustainable strategy and it won't lead to long-term success. I found out the hard way that busyness is definitely not the answer; it's a trap. I want to help you create the right strategies so that your business can grow without having to learn the hard way like I did.

Growth for your company begins when you can change the way you see yourself as a leader and create the kind of structures that can support sustainable growth for you and your company. With the right systems in place, your company will be able to weather any storm—any change—that comes your way.

CHAPTER 3

FOUNDATIONAL FAILURE

If your business feels like it's constantly on the verge of collapse and you feel like you're never getting ahead, it's not your fault. Most of us who work in the trades were taught how to fix problems related to our specific areas of expertise, but running a business takes a completely different set of skills. Whether you're aware of it or not, the way you're doing things right now might be hurting you more than helping you.

Let's take a look at some of the key problems you're likely facing to some degree. Every problem we discuss in this chapter stems from core issues that cause foundational failures. Your business is only as strong as its base. If that base is unsteady or unstable, everything built on top of it will collapse under the pressure. If not addressed, these challenges keep owners stuck, frustrated, and exhausted. This is why each and every one is addressed in the Leadership Playbook for the Trades, which we'll cover in Part 2.

Problem 1: I Don't Have ANY Time

No matter how much effort you put in, does it feel like your business always demands more from you? The workload never lightens, and you can't even imagine a day when this treadmill will stop. Even if you *know* you need a break, stepping away feels impossible. You feel anxious just thinking about it.

You have to find ways to give attention to your business and be available for clients when they call. In 1980, my dad got a call from a local candy factory in the middle of the night. This was early on, when he was a one-truck operation, before the additional business strains existed. He made the time and answered the call. He worked through the night, resolved their problem, and got the factory back up and running. That factory became one of his largest clients for *decades*—all because he made the time to show up when it mattered.

I've talked with some business owners who shared that they can't get to all their calls because they're too buried in the day-to-day chaos. If my father had passed on that one call, the opportunity at the candy factory and everything it ultimately brought would've passed him by. It's so important to free up enough time to seize opportunities when they come.

The consequences, if you don't find a way to make some time, are incredibly serious; missed work, strained relationships, divorce, declining health, and a growing sense of resentment toward the business you once really enjoyed. The first step is acknowledging that it cannot all rest on your shoulders. You don't get any more hours in your day. You have to be willing to find ways, through systems and people, to help lighten the workload so you can "create" more time.

Find tools that automate routine tasks, build systems to provide clarity, and then empower and train people you can trust so they can step in confidently when you need to step away. This is critical to regaining your time and your energy. When we get to Part 2, the Leadership Playbook for the Trades will give you some ideas about how to share the load to create more time in your day—all so you can focus on the things that can *grow* your business.

Self-Assessment: Does Your Business Own Your Time?
Use the questions below to honestly evaluate how much your

business is controlling your time, energy, and freedom. Rate yourself on a scale from 0 to 5 with 0 meaning "not accurate at all" and 5 meaning "most accurate."

Once you've rated yourself for each statement, total up your scores and then use the Answer Key to determine your next steps.

Success Check-in Statement	Self-Rating
I don't feel like I need to regularly work nights and weekends just to stay afloat.	
I feel I have enough time to spend with family and friends, pursue hobbies, and take vacations without the need to answer business calls or emails.	
I never feel guilty when I'm not working, I recognize that my downtime is good for me *and* the business.	
My business functions properly whether I am constantly involved in it or not.	
I can imagine a future where my workload decreases as I easily delegate tasks to others instead of taking them on myself.	
I never feel overwhelmed or stuck in a cycle of constant busyness.	
TOTAL UP YOUR SCORE:	

What Your Score Really Means

Score: 0 - 10
Owned by Your Business

Your business owns you. Immediate changes are necessary to reclaim your time and freedom. It's time for a complete reassessment of how you're operating. A healthy owner knows when to step back and set boundaries. This isn't about laziness—it's about survival. The first step toward regaining control is recognizing that your well-being is critical to your business's success. Schedule time for yourself and your family, and treat it as non-negotiable. Protecting your personal time is just as important as completing the next job. The Healthy Owner pillar in Chapters 5 and 11 will cover some strategies for making this easier to do.

Score: 11 - 20
Losing Control

Your business is heavily controlling your life. It's time to implement systems and empower others to take on more responsibility. Adjustments to delegation and/or time management could help. Delegating tasks and automating processes will allow you to focus on what only you can do: lead. Efficient operations mean fewer fires to put out, giving you time to breathe and strategize. Identifying repetitive tasks that can be automated or handed off to others can get you out of the daily grind. Getting to the clarity we'll talk about in Chapter 8 will help you find ways to delegate and prioritize, freeing up your time for higher-level decisions that only you can make.

Score: 21 - 30
Solid Foundation

Well done! You're on a solid foundation. Your business doesn't completely control your life and you're maintaining balance. You've established boundaries and created a business structure that allows you some breathing room. You've done some great work so far. Keep fine-tuning things. Clear Metrics, in Chapter 9, will remove the guesswork, allowing you to identify which tasks really need your attention at any given time. You'll stop wasting time on low-value work and focus on what drives growth.

Tracking your key metrics will help you determine where your time is most valuable so you can stop wasting energy on low-value tasks that don't move the needle.

Problem 2: I'm a Good Technician, but I Don't Know How to Lead

You've become a master in your trade. Whether it's plumbing, HVAC, or electrical work, fixing the problems that are put in front of you has become second nature. But running a business isn't the same as running a conduit or fixing a faucet. Results aren't as immediate, and solutions aren't always as clear.

If you've ever thought, "It's just easier if I do it myself," you're not alone. But thinking that way is a trap. It keeps you in the weeds and prevents you from focusing on the growth of your business. Leadership comes with its own challenges, and the skills that make you great in the field aren't the same ones it takes to lead effectively. That gap can feel overwhelming.

The reason the grass is greener on the "other side of the fence" is because it's just better maintained. I say this because fixing a problem in your trade is like cutting the grass, there's a sense of instant satisfaction. But leading a business is more like growing a healthy lawn. It takes time, care, and patience. It requires consistent effort over time, without the immediate feedback of a job well done. But, if you stick with it, what you get is definitely worth it.

To be a strong leader, you'll need to build a team and empower them to handle the tasks you are currently doing, create a culture where your employees thrive, and standardize processes so your team can operate without you. It's about learning to let go of control.

Standard Operating Procedures (SOPs), which we will talk more about in Chapter 4 and Chapter 7, will help you become more comfortable with delegating tasks to your team. SOPs help you replicate success in every task assigned so that every technician is handling the work with a cohesive approach. Writing out clear, step-by-step processes for common tasks ensures consistency and empowers your team to handle work without your constant oversight. SOPs allow you to scale your expertise across multiple technicians, freeing you to focus more on leading.

Self-Assessment: Are You Leading or Just Managing?

Use the questions below to help you evaluate your leadership capabilities and identify areas where you can grow. Honestly evaluate how comfortable and effective you are as a leader in your business or organization versus just managing the day-to-day. Rate yourself on a scale from 0 to 5 with 0 meaning "not accurate at all" and 5 meaning "most accurate."

Once you've rated yourself for each statement, total up your scores and then use the Answer Key to determine your next steps.

Success Check-in Statement	Self-Rating
I make good progress on any problems that come up without feeling like I'm constantly solving the same problems over and over.	
My "go-to" response when something needs to be done is to find someone and train them rather than saying I'll "just do it myself."	
I trust others to take the lead and solve problems that come up and regularly evaluate whether people on my team are in the right roles based on their skills and interests.	
I invest sufficient time in training and developing the skills of my people and have experienced team members who actively mentor and train those who have less experience.	

I have written SOPs for common tasks in my business and know my team is well trained and can handle their responsibilities effectively without being micromanaged.	
I dedicate adequate time to improving my leadership skills (e.g., reading applicable material, attending trainings, and seeking mentorship).	
TOTAL UP YOUR SCORE:	

What Your Score Really Means

Score: 0 - 10
Stuck in Technician Mode

You're doing too much yourself, which is likely making the process of creating any kind of growth a struggle. Start by delegating small tasks and building trust in your team. Create one SOP this week or delegate one task you currently handle yourself. Train and empower your team so you're not the only one solving problems. Leadership isn't about doing everything, it's about enabling others to succeed. The Skilled Technician pillar discussed in Chapter 7 will help you discover ways to recruit, develop, and retain the people you can trust in your business so you can focus on leading and get out of technician mode.

Score: 11 - 20
Struggling to Transition

You're making strides, but gaps remain. Prioritize building your SOPs and fostering mentorship on your team. It's an investment in their skills *and* in your freedom. Leadership requires trust. Once you've put these processes in place, you'll be able to trust that your team will step up. This isn't about abandoning oversight. It's about creating a framework for accountability.

SOPs can help you ensure consistency and quality. The Efficient Operations pillar in Chapter 8 can help you find ways to create repeatable processes that will support you and your team as you transition to a fully scalable business.

Score: 21 - 30
Strong Leadership Foundation

You've developed a solid foundation for leadership. Focus on documenting your processes and mentoring your team to maintain your momentum. You're no longer the one solving every problem; now, you're the one ensuring that your team has the tools, skills, and support to solve those problems themselves. Establish a mentorship system where experienced technicians train new hires. This creates a culture of shared knowledge and continuous learning, ensuring that your team can grow collectively. So, keep building your leadership mindset by creating SOPs and training programs. Next, work to get cultural buy-in from your team. Both Sticky Culture and SOPs will be talked about more in Part 2.

Problem 3: It's Too Hard to Find Good People

In the trades, competition to find and keep good people is fierce. Before hiring anyone, you'll want to first define the roles your business truly needs. Avoid vague job descriptions, so you know the skills required for every role, and what the responsibilities will be. When you have that information, you can attract the right candidates with the right qualifications. Then, you can focus on hiring not just for skill, but prioritize people who fit into your company culture. When you have a good company culture (like the Sticky Culture we'll talk about in Chapter 6 and Chapter 12), you will retain great employees and repel the toxic ones who kill morale and destroy the work environment.

Another antidote to the assumption that "you can't find good people" is that you can *develop* good people through strong training programs, mentorships, and apprenticeships. Training someone to work in the right key position can change everything. One of our technicians hated service work and customer interaction, yet he held a role that was very client facing and service heavy. The result was that he was frustrated and tense all the time, which caused him to keep making errors. He was a good fit with the company culture, but he was not in the right position. Once we shifted him to installations, a position that better aligned with his strengths, he was able to thrive and so was the business.

In the pillar of Skilled Technicians (Chapter 7), we'll talk about ways that will help you find, keep, and train good people.

Self-Assessment: Right People

This assessment can help you identify gaps in your hiring, training, and retention strategies. Use the questions below to honestly evaluate if you have (or could hire or develop) the right people in the right places within your organization. Rate yourself on a scale from 0 to 5 with 0 meaning "not accurate at all" and 5 meaning "most accurate."

Once you've rated yourself for each statement, total up your scores and then use the Answer Key to determine your next steps.

Success Check-in Statement	Self-Rating
Our job descriptions are written clearly, with specific skills and responsibilities outlined so that the correct people are put in the right positions.	
I find it easy to get good, available talent when I need to hire. I am able to prioritize cultural fit and values in our hiring process because they are clearly known.	

I trust my team to deliver results on their key performance indicators (KPIs). This makes my job easier so I am able to quickly redirect or address underperformance (as well as any negative behavior) on my team.	
I have structured training programs that develop employee skills. These options offer my people opportunities to see their work as careers and not just jobs.	
I help nurture employees in the job roles they are most interested in, offering them more satisfaction and providing the company with happier, more productive employees.	
Our workplace culture values employees and encourages loyalty. This causes the average employee retention rate to be significantly longer than competition in the area, saving my company money by having less employee turnover.	
TOTAL UP YOUR SCORE:	

What Your Score Really Means

Score: 0 - 10
Risk of Team Breakdown

You really don't have the right people, or your people aren't in the right places. Start with clearly defined roles and responsibilities for each of the positions in your company. That way, your team knows what they are supposed to be doing, what is important for the company, and why those activities are important. Then, whether it's with new or internal employees, you'll need training programs to help rebuild your team's foundation. Once the basics get put in place, many decisions about your people will become much clearer. You'll know if any changes need to be made, and if so, what they are. In Chapter 7, we'll look at the ways to set this up to make sure that you can build a strong team that won't break down.

Score: 11 - 20
Losing Control

With a score in this middle range, you are likely struggling to develop and retain the right team. You may have a star employee (or two) who understands your vision for the company enough to be able to cover some of the bases, but you may need to reassess your hiring practices. Keep yourself emotionally balanced so you can make clear, rational hiring decisions (until you can train other people to do the hiring) instead of reacting out of panic when you're short-staffed or you lose someone. You're on the right track, but improvements are needed so you won't feel like you're losing control. The Healthy Owner pillar in Chapter 5 will be a good start to set yourself up for success and meet others where they are.

Score: 21 - 30
Great Base for Great People

You've built a strong foundation for hiring, training, and retention. You might have several key employees that help keep things humming. Keep refining your training and culture initiatives to maintain that momentum. Attract and retain top talent by creating the type of environment that people want to get in and be a part of. Giving people deserved recognition, allowing them to have growth opportunities, and providing a positive workplace all matter to your team, so those things should matter to you as well. Focus on addressing and removing any toxicity. Then strengthen your training programs so that everyone can improve in their roles. The Skilled Technicians pillar in Chapter 7 can show you some new tools to help.

Problem 4: Cash Flow—Where Do I Even Start?

Cash flow is critical for your business. Managing it poorly is like having a leaky faucet that you can't stop. Most people in the trades aren't lucky enough to start out with $500,000 (or even $500) to be able to fund their dreams and help their business grow. Mostly, they start out with just enough cash to pay the bills. And, early in their business, the inconsistency of the work can feel like a big cycle of feast or famine in terms of their cash flow.

Labor, material, and marketing are three of the biggest expenses in the industry. You have to invest in all of these, at the right scale, in order to be able to grow effectively. It's a balancing act. You can't go all in on one without the others.

I know a business owner who invested in three shiny new trucks that he fully equipped with materials and tools, only to realize that they didn't have enough leads to bring in enough business to keep those trucks—and their technicians—busy. He hadn't been keeping track of information that would have told him whether purchasing the trucks made sense with the way his business was growing.

Even though the trucks were a great company asset, they just sat idle, draining cash flow. How about you, do you have any assets sitting idle? If yes, you too need to get tracking systems in place. In Chapter 9, we'll talk about the pillar of Clear Metrics which will show you the importance of knowing which metrics you should track to get back in balance in terms of how the business's cash flows to each of your biggest expenses.

Clear metrics also help you once you do have work coming in. You can track leading and lagging metrics (that is, future jobs on the books versus profitability on past jobs, which we'll talk more about in Chapter 9). This will help you make decisions about what to do next with clarity instead of relying only on gut instinct. Tracking the right metrics will help you see exactly where your money is currently going and where it should go. Because, trust me, you're not the only business owner lying awake at 2 AM worried about bills, payroll, and your dwindling energy reserves. I've been there too.

Keep monitoring the right metrics and adjusting as you go, and you'll find the balance you need to scale. It's not complicated, but that doesn't mean tracking your data is always easy. The Leadership Playbook for the Trades will show you steps you can take to help with all of this and more. The results will be worth the work. You'll get peace of mind.

Self-Assessment: Is Your Business Built on Stable Structures?

Use the questions below to honestly evaluate the systems and structures you have in place to manage cash flow. Then, use the responses to help you determine how well you know what steps to take and where to focus to effectively grow your business. Rate yourself on a scale from 0 to 5 with 0 meaning "not accurate at all" and 5 meaning "most accurate."

Once you've rated yourself for each statement, total up your scores and then use the Answer Key to determine your next steps.

Success Check-in Statement	Self-Rating
I know we have enough cash flow to make payroll and cover all our bills. I never feel like I'm just "making it up as I go" or "throwing money at problems" without a solid plan.	

I have a clear understanding of what my business needs most to grow right now. I know just how to prioritize which investments I make into my business.	
I know how to look at my lead metrics so that I can plan ahead for growth (and problems). I'm not stuck just reacting to what comes up.	
My customer service rep (CSR) knows how to prioritize calls as they come in and follow up as needed so we can close every job.	
I understand what my metrics are. I continuously focus on ways to improve efficiency at all levels.	
I have SOPs and/or workflows documented for my team. I review and update those processes regularly (at least quarterly).	
TOTAL UP YOUR SCORE:	

What Your Score Really Means

Score: 0 - 10
You're in Crisis Mode

Your business is at risk of operational failure. Start with mapping out your immediate priorities. You're likely unclear on them now, so you spend most of your time guessing or reacting. Strategic planning requires clarity and focus. A healthy mindset allows you to see the bigger picture. Before you can scale, you need clarity on your business's priorities. What are the immediate needs versus the long-term goals? For example, if your phones aren't being answered, hiring a customer service representative (CSR) might be more urgent than buying another truck. Also, you can't scale if you're doing everything yourself. Delegate tasks that don't require your direct involvement, and invest in tools and technology to automate repetitive processes. Scheduling software, project management platforms, and CRMs can save time and reduce errors. Many of these solutions will be covered in Part 2, where you'll learn how to implement them and what impact they can have.

Score: 11 - 20
Partial Control

You're on the right track, but you have some gaps to address. Your operations and systems are inconsistent, so you have trouble knowing how to deploy any money you *can* put together, and that's holding you back. Prioritize creating SOPs and automating key processes so that you can plan for future scalability. Strengthen your documentation and prepare your systems for future challenges. Once these are in place, you'll know what to invest in first and how to plan for growth. Think beyond your current team size or workload. Design your systems to support where your business will be in three to five years. This ensures your operations don't crumble under the weight of growth. The pillar of Efficient Operations in Chapter 8 will help you lay out these critical points of clarity.

Score: 21 - 30
Solid Foundation

You're operating quite efficiently! Continue tracking and refining your systems and structures to stay ahead of your future growth. SOPs are the backbone of creating a scalable business. They allow anyone in the organization to be able to understand how tasks are performed. And, SOPs ensure consistency for every job, every time, which is critical for maintaining quality as you continue to grow. Once systems are in place, you'll need to continuously evaluate them to ensure that they remain efficient. These systems may need to evolve as your business grows. Metrics are also critical to you being able to identify bottlenecks and improve processes in your business over time. Data-driven decisions can help you remove the guesswork. And this information will help you understand what's working and what isn't. Plus, it can help you know how to deploy what cash flow you have. When everything is well documented, it's easy to make informed decisions. You'll know what needs immediate attention. Metrics play a critical role here and that will be covered in the pillar of Clear Metrics in Chapter 9.

Problem 5: I Don't Think I Need Any Help

You're in the trades, so I understand the resistance to asking for help. Pride and independence are common traits, especially in trades industries. It's understandable. You've worked hard to get to where you are, and you're an expert in your trade, so asking for help feels like you're giving in to defeat.

But, this pride can be a double-edged sword. Initially, pride is what drove you to be able to start your business, become a master of your craft, and build something from the ground up. But that same pride can also be your downfall when it prevents you from getting help. I've seen it happen many times. The more burned out you become, the harder it is to see the forest for the trees. Stubbornness sets in, and instead of seeking guidance, you double down on the same exhausting path toward burnout by doing the same things—that clearly aren't working.

Your business was built on your back; with your blood, sweat, and tears. You take pride in solving problems, fixing things, and carrying the related loads. But absolutely no one—not even the very strongest among us—can carry everything. In your business, the longer you try to do it all on your own, the closer you come to breaking because of the pressure. It's that pressure that traps you in a cycle where asking for help feels like failure, even when it's the best (and sometimes the only) way out.

Living in your own echo chamber is common when you are trying to do everything on your own because you might start to believe that no one else understands your struggles. That isolation can lead you to be too overwhelmed to think straight, too stubborn to be able to delegate, and too exhausted to come up with any needed solutions. The business suffers, the relationships fray, and the dream you once had feels like a nightmare.

In the early years of my parents' business, there had been some tax trouble and my dad was on the brink of losing everything. Just days before the tax collectors came knocking, he took a plumbing job for a widow that turned into a massive, multi-day project. It got complicated and it was clear that he had underpriced it. He pushed on anyway, working tirelessly, almost to the point of collapse. In other words, he didn't ask for help. When he finally completed the job and gave her the new price, she paid the whole invoice. Dad and mom quickly took that check to the bank and were able to pay the tax collectors just enough to save the business from foreclosure to help our family. While this story was a win, it was also a big wake-up call for my parents.

You can't just keep pushing yourself to the brink of exhaustion and expect that there won't be any negative consequences. Sometimes, you just need help—financial, emotional, or operational.

The first step to solving your stubborn pride and independence is to acknowledge it exists. If you're lying awake at night going through checklists in your head, lashing out at employees or family members when everything is otherwise normal, or feeling absolute dread every morning when you think about going to work, you're burned out. And ignoring these warning signs won't make burnout go away, it will only make it worse. Experiencing burnout is not failure, it's a signal to let you know that something needs to change (and quickly).

Seeking help isn't a weakness; it's actually a strength. It allows you to grow and become a better leader, build a stronger and more resilient business, and get your life back. No one builds a successful business alone. You've got to surround yourself with good advisors, mentors, and support systems.

Isolation in that echo chamber you're in is another result of pride. Being able to connect with other business owners, peer groups, or a coach can provide invaluable support and perspective. Having the opportunity to share your challenges and learn from others will remind you that you're not alone. This support can help you see other solutions that might be within reach. This is why the pillar of Healthy Owner, in Chapter 5, is such a pivotal part of the Leadership Playbook for the Trades.

Self-Assessment: Are You Reaching Out More Than You're Burning Out?

Use the questions below to honestly evaluate how much you are able to seek out and get help in your business. Rate yourself on a scale from 0 to 5 with 0 meaning "not accurate at all" and 5 meaning "most accurate."

Once you've rated yourself for each statement, total up your scores and then use the Answer Key to determine your next steps.

Success Check-in Statement	Self-Rating
I never feel isolated or like there isn't anyone who understands my challenges. I have people I can talk to about any challenges I face.	
I'm never resistant to hiring outside help or seeking advice. I recognize that people outside of my position and outside of my company might have a clearer perspective. I regularly seek out that clarity.	

People never refer to me as stubborn.	
I surround myself with a supportive team. Team members feel free to provide suggestions for improving all aspects of our processes. I consider their suggestions for the company.	
I regularly seek advisors outside of my team for guidance, encouragement, or just to verify the decisions I am making within my organization.	
I use data to know how to move forward. This gives me the confidence to know where to ask for help and where to implement it.	
TOTAL UP YOUR SCORE:	

What Your Score Really Means

Score: 0 - 10
Lone Eagle

You are operating in isolation. This is having a negative effect on communication and cooperation inside your company or division. You're on the edge of collapse. It's time to reach out for help, re-evaluate your workload, and focus on regaining your balance. You're at a critical point. Prioritize your health, seek help, and re-examine how you're running your business. Severe burnout is on the horizon (if you're not already in the thick of it). Jump right to the pillar of Healthy Owner to get some ideas for how to better take care of yourself.

Score: 11 - 20
Moderate Yield

Sometimes you are actually able to reach out to ask for help with a task or two, but at this level, you probably still find it hard to get input on big-picture stuff. You are likely feeling mild to moderate burnout symptoms (or maybe more) and these symptoms of burnout might be impacting your decision-making abilities. Start addressing these early warning signs by delegating tasks so that you can make time for the tasks that only you can do. Take immediate steps to lighten your load and reach out for support. All five pillars in Part 2 will help you find ways to deal with and relinquish the tight grip you still have over much of your day-to-day business activities.

Score: 21 - 30
Not Too Proud to Build Something You Can Be Proud Of

Congratulations! A score in this range suggests that you are being very intentional and doing well in many key areas of leadership. You are able to remain open to help when and where it is needed for the best outcomes for your business. You've recognized that your biggest wins have come not from doing everything by yourself, but by sharing the struggles and the successes with others. You're not dictated by emotions when making decisions and can seek outside input to arrive at better outcomes. You likely feel motivated by your business and the possibilities it holds as you grow and scale. You are probably well liked by your team because of the support and encouragement you are able to pass along to them. Keep refining these skills to see continued growth and keep celebrating the related wins. The pillar of Sticky Culture in Chapter 6 provides ways you can continue to foster that empowered environment.

Recap

Building a strong foundation means embracing a mindset shift that moves from reactive to proactive and from surviving to thriving. None of this will happen overnight. It's a process you have to take one step at a time. It's easiest to start with the small things like answering the phone, training an employee, or setting a goal for something you can measure. Each step sets you up for long-term success. The Leadership Playbook for the Trades will show you some tools and strategies that you can implement right away to scale your company with confidence, knowing that every decision is building on the last toward a stronger and stronger business.

CHAPTER 4

PLAYBOOK OVERVIEW

There are five pillars in the Leadership Playbook for the Trades—Healthy Owner, Sticky Culture, Skilled Technicians, Efficient Operations, and Clear Metrics. In this chapter, I want to give you an overview of how all these pillars work together. Then, in Part 2, we'll take a deeper look at each of them individually. Finally, in Part 3, I'll leave you with some first steps to get you going on your journey.

The Big Picture

When I first introduce the framework to an owner, I always tell them it's about building a solid foundation so that they don't have the foundational failures we covered in the last chapter. Doing this foundational work assures they can grow their business in a sustainable way.

Each of the pillars is crucial to ensure that the business can operate smoothly, scale, and meet the owner's long-term goals.

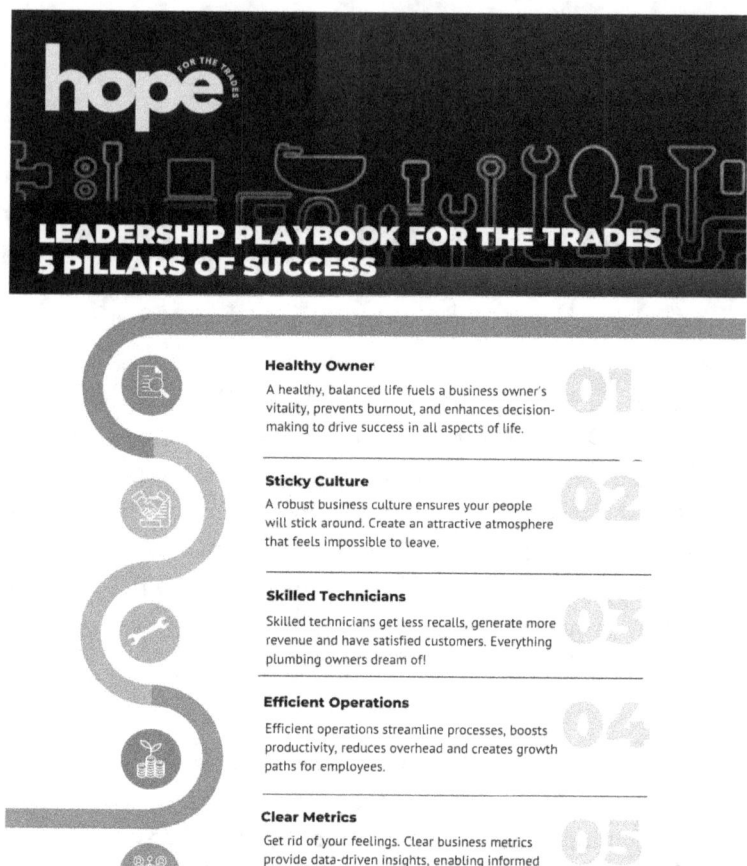

Healthy Owner

A healthy, balanced life fuels a business owner's vitality, prevents burnout, and enhances decision-making to drive success in all aspects of life.

01

Sticky Culture

A robust business culture ensures your people will stick around. Create an attractive atmosphere that feels impossible to leave.

02

Skilled Technicians

Skilled technicians get less recalls, generate more revenue and have satisfied customers. Everything plumbing owners dream of!

03

Efficient Operations

Efficient operations streamline processes, boosts productivity, reduces overhead and creates growth paths for employees.

04

Clear Metrics

Get rid of your feelings. Clear business metrics provide data-driven insights, enabling informed decisions, goal tracking, and continual improvement for strategic success.

05

OWN IT. SCALE IT. LEAD IT.

These five pieces don't work in isolation; they work together as an integrated whole. If one piece is weak, that weakness impacts the other pillars. For example, if your systems and operations are lacking, your people will struggle to execute in their roles effectively. If your culture isn't aligned, people won't buy into your vision, no matter how good your systems are. If your financial management is poor, even a solid culture and team won't be enough to keep the business afloat. And, if you aren't clear as the owner, as a *healthy* owner, then none of the other pieces of the business will function easily.

The key to the whole playbook is the balance and interplay between each pillar. This means constantly refining and improving each piece so that your business can grow peacefully and sustainably. That way you're not just chasing after the next big win or trying to put out the next big fire; you're intentionally building a business and a life you can be proud of.

How the Five Pillars Usually Start

1. **Healthy Owner**: When people come to me, they are often overworked and struggling with burnout. They're so caught up in the day-to-day operations that they neglect their personal well-being. They're wearing all the hats—CEO, CFO, HR, customer service, you name it. They're missing self-care routines, they don't have clarity about their life goals, and they lack the right mindset to scale in a way that is sustainable and manageable.

   A successful business starts with a balanced and resilient owner. A healthy owner takes care of themselves for the sake of the business if nothing else. They are emotionally stable and they have a long-term vision that reflects what matters most to them and will best support their business. By prioritizing their health and well-being, establishing meaningful goals, and creating a strategic plan for the future, a healthy owner lays a solid foundation for effective leadership. Dialing this in allows you to lead with clarity and stability, which sets an example for your team and builds a legacy that aligns with your values. We'll visit this pillar in the next chapter.

2. **Sticky Culture**: People are your greatest asset yet many business owners don't realize how crucial culture is until

it's too late. They've been overly focused on growth and operations, leaving culture to evolve haphazardly. In the worst cases, they've inherited a toxic culture that hasn't been shaped intentionally. They're missing clear values and team alignment. They have no framework for creating a positive, productive work environment.

Creating a sticky culture means cultivating a workplace that attracts, engages, and retains top talent. It means having structured engagement to foster trust and being able to lead with what truly matters to employees. When team members feel valued and connected to the company's mission, they are more committed to delivering excellent service. By consistently reinforcing your company's values, you can maintain open communication and offer more personalized growth opportunities. In that way, your business builds a loyal, motivated team that reflects the company's commitment to those values. Chapters 6 and 7 will cover both sticky culture and skilled technicians to find ways to help serve your people.

3. **Skilled Technicians**: Business owners often have a small but effective team early on, but as they scale, they struggle to create the right leadership structure and hire the right people. Sometimes, they don't have an organized hiring process or they've failed to delegate effectively, leaving them bogged down in too many roles. They need to create defined roles, leadership training, and a hiring process that fits the business's needs.

Skilled technicians are the cornerstone of a successful service business. The focus here is on recruiting talented technicians, investing in structured training and development programs, and helping technicians find the right roles for them. Setting up comprehensive training, including SOPs, mentorship programs, and skill specialization tracks, allows technicians to deliver high-quality service which then fosters customer trust and satisfaction. Developing and retaining skilled technicians allows your business to create a reputation for excellence that can set your business apart within your industry. This will be covered in Chapter 7, Skilled Technicians.

4. **Efficient Operations**: Most small businesses, especially during the startup phase, don't have formalized systems in place. It can all be very ad-hoc, depending on who's available and what seems to work at the time. As the company grows, this often leads to chaos and breakdowns. To stay efficient, you need clear SOPs, repeatable processes, and systems that make it easier to automate and delegate work.

Efficient operations are essential to achieve scalable growth and profitability. They help you establish clear roles and responsibilities, develop robust systems and processes, and implement balanced marketing strategies. This will help you create a forward-looking organizational chart, centralize operational tasks, and build a marketing strategy that combines digital and grassroots efforts—all designed to streamline the company's workflow. Documentation is crucial because it ensures consistency, accountability, and adaptability as the business scales. Put together, these operational structures allow your business to handle higher job volumes without having to compromise on service quality. We'll discuss more about these standards in Chapter 8.

5. **Clear Metrics**: This pillar is built to handle financial management methods and Key Performance Indicators (KPIs). It tends to be limited or missing in about 90% of the businesses I work with. These owners have little to no financial clarity. Either they don't track their numbers at all, or the numbers they do track are vague, which means they can't take action based on them. This keeps them from moving the needle in their business. Some have QuickBooks

but don't understand how to pull insights from it. Others are just guessing about margins, profitability, and cash flow. You need accurate financial reports (like statements for profit and loss) and clear KPIs. You also need an understanding of key metrics and some type of dashboard to monitor all of these data points regularly.

Data-driven decisions are the key to continuous improvement. Having clear metrics helps you establish meaningful KPIs, differentiate between leading and lagging indicators, and use your actual metrics to guide your business's growth. By asking the right questions, defining the KPIs that align with your company's goals, and understanding the story behind the data, you can track your progress effectively. You can then learn to use the data to make better decisions rather than freaking out because you don't know how to respond. Staying balanced while processing key data, rather than reacting or overreacting to every minor fluctuation, fosters a culture of improvement and agility. At the same time, regularly reviewing and refining your strategies based on what you learn from your metrics enables your business to stay aligned with its vision. These informed adjustments can then support sustainable, long-term success. Chapter 9 will talk more about the pivotal part these metrics play.

The Playbook as Your Partner

Thus far, we've talked about the pain points you're facing. You may have already had an aha moment or two as you read through the first part of this book. As I work with owners in the trades, they often say to me, "The answer was right in front of me, and I knew it, but it didn't feel clear." When I use ideas from the playbook to connect the dots for them in their business, it's like a lightbulb goes off and they wonder how they hadn't seen this pattern or issue. It's just human nature to get stuck in your own "box" or live inside that echo chamber (which was one of the common problems we discussed in Chapter 3). With that being said, I want you to know that this isn't your fault. You needed more information to see the transformation your business needs, and now you're going to have it.

Earlier you met my friend and business partner, Luke. He and I have this "two in the box" mentality when we discuss any issues. We have different ideas, but we complement each other perfectly. We might argue, but we always have a strong foundation and we're aligned on what matters. That stability creates a safe space for working through any decision.

The stability I have in my partnership with Luke is what I want the Leadership Playbook for the Trades to provide for you. It's here to provide clarity, give you direction, and help you do things at the right pace and at the right time—allowing you to build your business in a sustainable manner no matter what comes your way.

This playbook can give you ideas to create better structure. It's really hard to find clarity when you're in the weeds; it can be easy to get lost in the day-to-day. Having someone walk alongside you, to help you see things from a more neutral perspective, is invaluable. When you *don't* have a consultant or partner, the playbook can feel like someone's walking this strategic path with you while you sort through the weeds. The idea is to provide guidance that you can apply to immediate issues, so you can hold on to what you learn. That's the essence of it.

Now, let's look at two examples where the playbook has helped other trade business owners just like you.

Example 1: Van or No Van

I was working with a woman who was feeling overwhelmed by the pressure of the slow season. She told me, "I have all these bills, but the phone's not ringing because we're in a beach town, and it's slower now. I'm thinking about taking out a loan just to cover some bills and also buy a van." She continued by saying, "I almost did it already, but I wanted to see what you'd say first since I haven't talked to you in a week." She shared that she thought I would just say yes and tell her to "go for it."

But when we talked about it, I told her that buying a van at that moment could be a very dangerous decision for her business. It was a 13% loan with no real plan behind it and it wouldn't generate any income. She was so focused on the bills right in front of her. While she didn't have any debt, money also wasn't coming in, so I helped her acknowledge that. I didn't say anything amazing—I just helped provide clarity for her situation and reminded her where she had come from and where she said she wants to go in the future. She may still get a van at some point, but that wasn't the right time or the right way to spend money just then. I could see her relief as I supported her in making the decision that made the most sense for where she was in her business at the time.

It's really common for a trade business to experience slow seasons—especially in certain industries. In the trades, unless you're doing high-demand services in an area of dense population without any seasonality, the work can be inconsistent. And even if you're not in a slow season, it could still be inconsistent in terms of getting paid by your customers' general contractors. That kind of fluctuation seems hard to escape.

What you're after here is sustainability, a business that can withstand all the ups and downs, including the slow seasons, and still be resilient. That's really what you want to build.

The biggest value you'll get in this book is understanding that what got you here isn't necessarily what will get you where you want to go. There's so much that you already *know*, but the playbook can give you the perspective you need to move forward.

In this case, the client I was working with just needed to visit her clear metrics (more in Chapter 9) and they would've shown the data she needed to base her decision on.

Example 2: Phones Versus "Cleaning House"

I once worked with a one-man shop that had gotten up to eight men, lost it all, and went back to being a one-man shop. The owner came to me, contemplating if he should stay in plumbing or go work for somebody else. Months passed as he pondered that.

I took him through questions like, "Do you want to be in this? What would it look like if you were motivated to keep your business? Where do you feel gifted?" I was trying to help him connect the dots. His answers to those questions led him to the conclusion that he still wanted to be working in the field. He enjoyed the work and still wanted to be *in* his own plumbing business. So, he still takes calls three days per week.

Once that decision was made, to grow, he needed to create a goal for the business and then write it down. He had to move past the *theory* of being in business to create a strategic plan, and then put down a goal. For him, the goal was to "clean house." There was some organizing that had to be done with the phones and communication, his warehouse was a mess, his vans were disorganized, and he had stuff that was 30 years old that hadn't been cleaned up. He said, "I can't even bring somebody into my business to hire them because I would be embarrassed to do an interview here. Plus, I don't have a van ready for them."

So, he had the goal of cleaning house for two months, and he was slowly working toward it. But then, he suddenly sends me a long email talking about why the phone's not ringing, and he's getting worried, saying he has got to get more calls and do more work. I just wrote back, "What's the goal? The goal has been to clean house. Are we switching it to make the phone ring, to generate a lot of work, and hire people?"

When we met again, I asked him to tell me *why* the goal was to clean house. He went through all the reasons, and I asked if he still believed those reasons. He said, "Yes." So, I said, "Okay, then what do we need to do? Do we need to make the phone ring, or do we clean house?" With his renewed confidence and clarity, he said, "We need to clean house because I can't take on more work, and I can't get more guys until that's done."

In this example, the owner and I had worked through the concepts in the pillar of Healthy Owner to get him started. Then he had to set up systems and responsibilities for efficient operations to keep moving forward a step at a time. Only then could he bring in more work.

The concepts in the playbook are about bringing you back to what you know, keeping you on track, and showing you accountability. You can use the playbook to guide your decisions and then revisit them as you go. You'll want to find a way to implement your own accountability. Find a friend, a colleague, or even a family member, and when you decide what you will be working on first after going through the playbook, have them hold you to it. Then, go back to the playbook and get on to the next steps.

Recap

If you follow the framework exactly, you will get clarity, first and foremost. When you're in business, and you're putting out fires all the time—especially when growing and scaling—the smoke from all those fires can blind you to what's right in front of you. The Leadership Playbook for the Trades can help you see how to cut through all that and give you clear, actionable steps.

As you embark on this journey, remember that growth is not a one-size-fits-all process. You'll want to use the playbook as a flexible guide, adapting its strategies to meet the unique needs of your business. It can be a partner to you as you bring in these new and updated concepts. As your business grows, so will your approach to leadership, operations, and customer service. This playbook is here to support you along the way, helping you build a business that is not only profitable but resilient and respected.

If, after reading this chapter, you're thinking, "If I could just have someone guide me…" reach out. We would be honored to come alongside you to help guide you to your goals. If you want to dig more deeply into each of the pillars, read on as that's what we'll cover over the next five chapters.

PART 2
The Pillars of the Playbook
(Your New "Tools of the Trade")

CHAPTER 5

HEALTHY OWNER

Nobody's Dying!

Running a business in the trades can feel like a never-ending series of emergencies: clients calling in a panic, staff calling in sick or not showing up, equipment shortages, operational trouble. And, that's just to handle what comes in new every day, that doesn't take into account the ongoing business side of things like payroll, ordering, insurance, and workers' comp. I know because I've been there. The pressure can make every day feel like a 911 situation.

But, here's the thing--nobody's dying.

Saying that might sound dismissive because it sure as heck *feels* like everything is critical in your business. But, if you can take a step back and realize that not every problem is your personal burden to fix, you'll recognize that statement—nobody's dying—is true.

In this chapter, we'll take a deeper look at the importance of the first pillar in the Leadership Playbook for the Trades—**Healthy Owner**. This is where it all begins. So, since this is our first day at *this* job, let's go back to the beginning and kick off where every plumber starts on their first day—with the three rules of plumbing:

- Rule #1: Shit flows downhill,
- Rule #2: Don't bite your fingernails, and

- Rule #3: Payday is on Friday.

Because we're a plumbing family and recognize just how important rule #1 is, "shit" is actually an exception to the non-swearing rule in our house, of course only in the right context. For this pillar, you have to accept your position—you're an owner. And, as an owner, you've got to take a step back to lead—you've got to get yourself from the bottom of that hill. I've found that one of the hardest lessons for business owners to learn is that not everything can be on you. Too many owners try to swoop in to "save the day," but that can't scale.

As mentioned in previous chapters, lots of people in the trades spend their time putting out fires, and I've often said that my dad was the very best "firefighter" we had. I remember watching him jump into action immediately with his metaphorical fireman's hat on so he could fix whatever problem came up. And the truth of the matter is, people loved him for that. He had energy and drive. He was the guy everyone could rely on in a crisis. But it took a toll on him. I watched how that approach impacted his life and health, and I knew I had to do things differently. I realized pretty quickly that I couldn't be a "firefighter" like my dad, nor would I be as good at it as he was.

We're in the trades; we're not doctors in the ER, first responders, or firefighters answering a call. The trades are important, and the troubles we address are real, but we can't treat every issue like it's life or death. We can't make clear decisions at the bottom of the hill, and we must stop letting our businesses dictate our lives and define who we are!

The business needs you to provide direction, clarity, and leadership. It needs you to know what's most important and what a balanced life looks like for you. The business needs you to separate yourself from the organization as a whole enough to allow others to rise and come alongside you. Your business needs you to be a healthy owner.

Five Things Needed for a Peaceful Business

There are five things that every trades owner needs to know how to do to create a peaceful business that's capable of growth, and **you becoming a healthy owner is the secret key that makes these things possible**. Until you know the truth of who you are, you won't see where you are or know where you want to go.

Embrace Humility

Humility will challenge you to put your ego aside and get honest about where you are and what your priorities are. Then, you'll know how to confront any trade-offs. It's okay to want financial success and time freedom. Or to want to step away from the day-to-day grind. Just know that achieving financial independence or time freedom might mean delegating tasks or letting go of control, and that's a big leap for many owners. But hopefully, by this point in the book, you are ready to embrace the idea that you can't do this all on your own. You've got to get humble enough to recognize when you need help and that others can do a job as well as—and sometimes, even better than—you.

This isn't just my idea, the Bible talks about how the humble are blessed and how they shall inherit the earth. This is the secret to success. When pride boasts about how *you* created this or that or how *you* accomplished these big things on your own, that success can be hollow and fleeting.

As a healthy owner, you'll be able to embrace humility to stay grounded and able to adapt. Let's face it, just like I alluded to in Chapter 2, shit happens. The market changes, people die, employees leave, or maybe a pandemic throws the entire world into chaos. When things don't go as planned, without humility, it's easy to become defensive and inflexible. But with humility, you can step back, reevaluate, and make adjustments. You're more open to different options, and you can keep your eyes on the goals you have for your company and your life.

Humility reminds you that neither business nor life are really about finding a perfect ending, they're about progress toward your goals. Healthy owners are humble enough to stay open to new ideas, recognize they need the support of others, and continuously look for opportunities to improve. Here are five ways to be more humble.

- Be aware of not just your strengths but also your shortcomings and limitations.
- Be able to recognize and acknowledge the strengths of others.
- Be open to learning from and adapting with your employees and colleagues.
- Work towards putting the needs of others before your own, which will ultimately get you more of what you want as well.
- Become a good listener and make sure others feel heard and understood by you.

This likely doesn't come naturally since the trades are generally considered a "tear-down" culture where it's every man for himself and people tear down others while trying to make themselves look good. But what matters now is your willingness to learn, adapt, and seek guidance. It takes humility to be able to pause and reflect, but doing so can help you see where and how your current approach might not be working.

The pillar of Healthy Owner really begins with taking time to create space for yourself to define (and then continue to redefine) what success looks like for you. Humility allows you to take out the ego and focus on what truly matters. This isn't about proving what you can handle, it's about building something bigger than yourself.

It takes an honest recognition of our own worth and the worth of others to truly succeed.

Humility is the key, and accountability is the means to get there. As a healthy owner, humility is what will allow you to seek support in the form of this book, as well as any coaches or mentors you might choose to work with. Then, accountability can help keep you on track. (Accountability is actually important through every facet of your business, so we'll talk more about that in the pillars of Efficient Operations and Clear Metrics in Chapters 8 and 9.)

Hire Smarter

You know the old saying, "If you want something done right, do it yourself." But living fully in that mindset leads to micromanagement, missed opportunities, and ultimately burnout. That approach can destroy your business and likely take you down with it.

Hiring smarter isn't just about pulling warm bodies off the street. A healthy owner knows that it starts with acknowledging your own limitations. You need talented people to help you grow. And this may be hard to hear, but you're not great at everything. There are people who can do some things better than you, and that's okay.

So, instead of hiring people who think just like you, focus on looking for team members who complement your strengths and fill in your knowledge and skill set gaps. You need to know yourself well enough to recognize what those gaps are. It takes a healthy owner to have that vision.

Better hiring starts by defining the roles, responsibilities, and success metrics upfront so you and the candidate know exactly what's expected. For example, when hiring a technician, you can't just say, "We need to hire someone." You'll want to outline what specific tasks they'll perform, what systems they'll use, and the KPIs they'll be measured against. This way, you avoid having frustrated employees who aren't meeting expectations that they never knew existed in the first place.

A healthy owner also knows that culture is even more critical than technical aptitude. Hiring smarter means prioritizing candidates who fit the culture you want to build, even if they lack certain technical skills. For example, if your company values teamwork, look for people who demonstrated collaboration in their previous roles. If your business is built on trust and reliability, you'll want to hire individuals with a proven track record of accountability. Often, you can hire for culture and train for skills, because character is much harder to develop.

And, even the best hires need onboarding support, training or mentorship, and opportunities to grow. You can't expect them to excel without guidance. Create the structures they'll need for success rather than just thinking they are there to solve all your problems. You don't just hire someone to do a job. you invest in their potential to grow your business.

The pillar of Healthy Owner allows you to surround yourself with capable, aligned people so you can create a business that doesn't rely on just you to be able to function. That's the ultimate goal—a business that runs smoothly because you've hired smarter by finding people who share your mission, vision, and values. You'll also learn how to invest in onboarding new employees to set your new hires up for success with training and clear expectations (through Skilled Technicians in Chapter 7). Plus, you'll teach them how to use your KPIs to track their progress (through Clear Metrics in Chapter 9). It all works together, and becoming a healthy owner is how it starts.

Raise Up Leaders

To raise up leaders, you must shift your mindset from being "the boss" to being more of a coach or a mentor. A healthy owner recognizes that their job isn't to have all the answers, it's to steer others to find answers themselves. As your business grows, you'll need to empower others so that they can step up and lead. I'm not talking about relinquishing control, I'm talking about sharing responsibilities and creating opportunities for your team to grow.

You'll identify leadership potential by looking for team members who show initiative, problem-solving skills, and a willingness to learn. Sharing your knowledge and experience can help them succeed. Instead of waiting for them to "prove" themselves, you can start by giving them a small leadership role—maybe managing a project or mentoring a junior technician. You provide guidance and feedback but allow them the freedom to make and learn from their own decisions.

Over time, you can expand their responsibilities, offering more complex challenges and greater autonomy. You celebrate their successes, help them learn, and encourage them to share their insights with others. Eventually, they become confident in their own leadership skills and not only support your business; they also inspire others to follow in their footsteps.

As a healthy owner, if you can delegate with trust and allow your people to lead, you'll be able to let go of micromanaging and trust your team to find a way to rise to each challenge. If your people can't handle things without you, the problem isn't with them. It's with you. That may sting a little, but you've got to be able to step back and have your systems and people handle what arises. They may not do it as perfectly as you right away, but they can only figure out how to move forward if they're allowed to try. Remember, nobody's dying, so you can always go back and fix something if you need to.

Raising up leaders is the *ultimate multiplier*. When you've invested in leadership development, you can build a stronger team and create a legacy. The long-term success of your business hinges on your ability to raise up leaders who can take ownership, move the company forward, and inspire others. The leaders you develop will carry your vision forward, even when you're not in the room. This isn't a task you can delegate to HR or complete with just a training manual. It's a daily practice that starts with a healthy owner. It's you who creates a culture where leadership can flourish. And that builds the foundation for scaling your business sustainably and running it peacefully.

Have the Heart of a Servant

"Whoever wants to be great must first become a servant."
Matthew 20:26 (MSG)

Having the heart of a servant shifts your focus from "What's in it for me?" to "How can I best serve others?" As a healthy owner, you'll be able to put the needs of your team above your own to focus on how you can support their growth. Some great ways to start are:

- Actively listen when your team is sharing challenges, aspirations, or feedback.
- Find ways to remove obstacles like old or outdated processes or equipment to ease their frustrations.
- Be the kind of leader who your team aspires to become. Show them what it looks like to prioritize your own health, care for the team's health, commit to excellent customer service, and follow through on your promises.

When you have the heart of a servant, you create a culture where employees feel valued, supported, and empowered to succeed. You want to approach every interaction from a mindset of service, especially when your team or your customers are facing challenges. This will help you build trust and loyalty by consistently delivering excellent service and treating clients and employees with compassion.

The trades are in the business of service—we solve problems, ease stress, and improve the lives of our customers.

To truly thrive though, your service mindset must extend beyond your clients to your employees, your community, and even to yourself. When an owner is healthy, having the heart of a servant becomes the way to transform leadership into something truly impactful.

Another tradesman shared that as he pulled into his business's parking lot and saw seven cars, it hit him—he was being asked to lead and support seven families. He recognized the impact of his servant's heart, and his responsibility for the health and well-being of all these other people. How many cars are in your parking lot? How many people do you support? These are the very people you want to bring along with you in your success.

As a healthy owner with the heart of a servant, you'll see the effects of your leadership on your people, your customers, and your community. Let's look at how this plays out.

1. **Your People.** Employees are the backbone of your business. When you focus more on how you can serve your team, they focus on how they can best serve your clients.

2. **Your Customers.** At the end of the day, your business exists to serve customers. Having the heart of a servant drives you to see beyond transactions and focus on building relationships with your clients.

3. **Your Community.** Giving back to the community might mean participating in local events, supporting charitable causes, or offering free services to those in need. You are part

of a larger whole and you contributing with the heart of a servant strengthens everyone around you.

The heart of a servant is the bridge between humility and strong leadership. A healthy owner grounds their actions in empathy and care, ensuring that every decision made benefits the people served. This approach doesn't just create a thriving business. It creates a legacy of trust, loyalty, and impact. By leading with a servant's heart, you build stronger relationships, inspire greater commitment, and create a culture where everyone feels valued. Whether it's by understanding an employee's career goals or a customer's frustrations, empathy builds trust and loyalty. People want to work for and buy from leaders who genuinely care about them.

Know Your Mission, Vision, and Values

Whether you've taken the time to define them or not, your mission, vision, and values drive your business. They provide answers to the most foundational questions; why, where, and how. Why is there a business, where is it going, and how will the business be conducted? An owner must be healthy enough to answer these questions with honesty and authenticity. This is where the pillar of Healthy Owner comes in.

A business without clearly defined mission, vision, and values is like a ship without a compass. It might move, but it has no guiding direction. I've found the concepts of mission, vision, and values to be missing in most trade companies. These are the principles that can help clarify your decision-making, align your team, and set your business apart in your industry.

It takes a healthy owner to be able to create and embrace these guiding principles. You need to allow for self-reflection, honest assessment, and the acknowledgment that your business exists for a purpose that's more than just bringing in revenue. Mission, vision, and values aren't just grand goals, they should be practical tools that guide every aspect of your business.

Mission: Why Are You in Business?

Why does your business exist? What problem does it solve? Who does your company serve? There are already hundreds of people who talk about corporate missions—we're not trying to reinvent the wheel here. You just need to answer the fundamental question of why your business exists. And no, the answer isn't just "to make money."

Every trade business serves a purpose beyond the financials. Whether it's solving problems for customers, creating jobs, or improving the community, your mission should capture your deeper "why." And the truth is, you may need to start with your own personal "why." I had a client who just couldn't get clear and move forward with his business until he could figure out his personal "why."

When you become a healthy owner, you'll be able to step back and reflect on the true purpose of your business. You'll be able to craft a mission that resonates with your team, inspire your customers, and contribute to your community. When you take the time to define your mission, you align your business with a purpose greater than yourself.

Vision: Where Are You Going?

Where do you see your company in the future? How will it actually accomplish the mission you just wrote? What influence will it have on the trade that you're in, on the community you're serving, and on the customers and employees you're impacting?

Your vision lets you and everyone you work with know where you are headed. It's the big picture of what you want your business to achieve and the impact you want to have. Vision is aspirational, forward-looking, and should be motivating.

Healthy owners dream big while staying grounded in reality. A true vision is about creating a business that leaves a positive and lasting impact. A healthy leader isn't afraid to admit they need help and they will encourage collaboration. Involving your team and seeking their input can help you create a shared goal that everyone can rally behind.

Values: How Will You Get There?

Values are the principles that guide and support your business operations as well as your life. They act as your moral compass. Your values shape your decisions, and these values and decisions are what shape the culture of your company so that you can live out your mission and vision.

We again start with you as the leader, the healthy owner. You need a personal mission and values. I often say this looks like a eulogy statement. What would you want people to say at your funeral? Why do you exist, what are your God-given talents, how do you want to serve others (as a parent, a plumber, a friend, a church member, etc.)? What problems can you help with, who can you help, and who do you see yourself becoming? How do you want to impact the world around you? You get one shot. You are here with these specific people at this specific time. This is why it is so important to think about which values will guide you as you move through this life.

The values you choose define the behaviors, attitudes, and priorities that drive you and your business forward. It's easy to use buzzwords like "excellence" or "innovation," but a healthy owner reflects more deeply on what truly matters. What do you want to be known for? Where do you refuse to compromise? Do you value trustworthiness, empathy, care, collaboration, teamwork, compassion, accountability, giving back, or something else?

When your values are built from a place of true introspection, you'll not only define what your company stands for. You'll also ensure your operations reflect those principles. They're not just aspirations. Take action on the values that matter most to you every day. The pillar of Healthy Owner makes this possible.

Living Your Mission, Vision, and Values

Defining your mission, vision, and values, both personally and professionally, is only the first step. The real work comes in living them out every day. They aren't just words framed up on a wall. They're the foundation of your company culture and should be the criteria for every decision you make. Defining yourself as a healthy owner keeps you grounded, reminding you that your business is about serving others. It allows you to engage your team in the process, accept feedback, and stay true to your principles, even when that feels challenging.

When mission, vision, and values become the heart and soul of your business, they drive growth, foster trust, and create a legacy that lasts.

Recap

Becoming a healthy owner doesn't automatically guarantee success, but it does guarantee peace. Developing the skills of a healthy owner puts you in a position to tie all these practices together. It's what allows you to step back, gain perspective, and build a business that's not just successful but also meaningful. Once you truly know who you are, you'll find it easier to embrace humility, hire smarter, raise up leaders, have the heart of a servant, and align your business with your mission, vision, and values. When all that's in place, you and your business will have more peace and be in a position to accomplish more than you can even imagine.

Even if it's all you do, becoming a healthy owner will still get you 80% of the way to a more peaceful, more profitable business. It will help you get "up the hill," afford you a new perspective, and allow you to embrace more of the options that are available.

Getting connected to your "why" and focusing on progress will make it possible for you to build a business—and a life—you can be proud of. Consider reviewing these concepts every few months to track your progress and identify new opportunities for growth. And when things get tough—remember, when it comes to the intense moments that will arise while showing up faithfully to serve your clients, *nobody's dying*. Take some deep breaths, remember what matters most, and create the time and space you need.

CHAPTER 6

STICKY CULTURE

It Doesn't Have to Be Hard—Just Sticky

Many owners feel like once they "see the light" of being a healthy owner, the next step is to jump in and set up how the business is laid out. I thought the same thing, but after my mom got sick and I took over the company, I quickly learned that you can't just make operational changes without getting your culture right first. The way my dad had the business set up as a mom-and-pop shop was all I knew at the time, so I thought the culture was fine.

But, I learned that what I had "inherited" did not have a culture that could support the kind of growth we were aspiring to. Just like our company *had* a culture when I inherited it, your company *has* a culture too, whether or not you are aware of it. But, you can become more deliberate about the choices you make to consciously create a workplace where people want to "stick" around. So, **Sticky Culture** is the next step in the playbook.

So, What Is Culture?

Your people (including you) and how they work together creates the culture of your company. In many trade companies, there seems to be a bit of a misunderstanding around culture. Many business owners think that holding a Christmas party once a year is a sufficient practice to "build company culture," but that's just surface-level work.

Other times, owners think, *Since I gave you a job, you should be thankful.* That thinking doesn't really show care to your people in the way *they* truly want to be cared for. Their lives are not just about their jobs. Everybody has to have a job and they may recognize that having their job is an opportunity. But they don't see it as you doing them a favor, and that type of thinking doesn't create a sticky culture.

Setting up a sticky culture from the beginning allows you to drop people in or raise people up in the organization as it grows, while everything in the culture stays rooted in the things you define as important. You're not trying to rebuild the foundation every time you grow or add a new person. If you have the systems and structure to support them, then as you scale, you don't have to stop and try to rebuild from the bottom up each time you enter a new stage of growth.

Making Culture Sticky

When you build a workplace that considers care beyond the 40 hours of the workweek, that's when culture really starts to get sticky. A sticky culture is one that attends to the whole employee—the attitudes of the team members working there are positive and they are caring and inclusive enough that people spend their whole careers there.

Your culture, when it has defined core values and everyone knows where they fit in the company—and how it all works together—can create the kind of stickiness and atmosphere that brings in new talent too. With everything laid out, you'll be able to figure out pretty quickly if someone you hire might be a good fit.

Organizational charts, as well as roles and responsibilities, are often absent or poorly designed in many trade companies. Things are typically chaotic, with vague ideas of who holds what roles and how they are meant to perform in that role. This may work without damaging culture for a time while the company is small enough that everyone can see everyone else. But as a business grows with these critical systems missing, tasks get dropped or lost, and people start trying to point fingers. That's not good for company culture. Clarity helps maintain the culture of your company by allowing everyone to understand the team, the players, and how the different pieces work together.

For example, I tell my hiring manager to come from the mindset of hiring two people and only keeping one. Why? Because so often, even though both new hires may be skilled, only one of them might live into our values and fit our culture. Our good culture polices itself because people love it. Our techs will let us know when someone is green and needs more training, but they will *spotlight* someone who isn't trying to live into the values of our company. They know how hard we've worked for our good culture and the benefits they receive from it, and they don't want that culture to be negatively affected or have it disappear.

Beyond setting up a good internal company structure, there are many other ways to meet the needs of your employees, including:

- Good healthcare
- Flexible personal time off (PTO)
- Remote working opportunities
- Company gatherings
- Breakfast in the mornings or grab and go snacks available
- Strategic ways to give words of affirmation

It doesn't have to be over the top. Technicians can't expect a manager or someone to text them saying, "Wow, awesome job clearing out that toilet. That was incredible. We need more people like you." No. But you, as the owner or manager, can text them when they go above and beyond on a job, when they pick up someone else's slack, or even on their birthday to thank them for being an incredible employee and for the privilege of working with them.

My project managers invest in our people, build relationships, and show appreciation. For example, I saw a manager and a tech go out for a steak dinner the other night just to connect and build the relational side of things, not just to work out the next job. Managers can buy hand warmers and a hot lunch for their team members who will be out on a cold day. There are little touches along the way that can remind your team that you care, that you see them, and that they are important to you and the business. This helps to solidify why our company is a better place to work than someplace else. This is not something the company *has* to do, but things like the examples I shared can create the kind of sticky culture for people that says we're different from our competition.

A Cautionary Tale

A manager I work with from another company has an overly militant boss who's very cut-and-dried. He thinks his ideas should take priority and be implemented immediately. This makes the manager's job very difficult when he's working on department goals and trying to lead the people under him. One second he has the autonomy to run the department, and the next, the rug is pulled out from under him and he's forced to change course. That narrow-mindedness squelches people's creativity.

You may *say* your people are empowered, but you've actually limited and boxed them in when you force your new ideas or agendas on them. This must be a team effort. People aren't just robots that move on command. It's fine to create a process or a customer experience that you want (actually, it's very good to have clear processes), especially for your technicians. But, if you micromanage your team or force your priorities to take precedence, your people will revolt and you will create a culture that is far from sticky.

Not every tech is going to say the script exactly the same, look exactly the same, organize their truck like you would, do every job the way you've written it, or introduce an upsell exactly how you said they should. They are humans with God-given differences. So, we build a healthy structure and put good boundaries around it to live into our mission and our vision, but then we allow our people to have some freedom to innovate and be who they are. It is important to define the processes, metrics, and accountability markers to create the boundary (fence) that allows people to follow the rules but also lets them be themselves. That's when they're finally able to live out their unique gifts within the boundaries and still accomplish the work you have for them.

Yes, we're all plumbers, electricians, carpenters, or HVAC people, but even within that scope, we're all uniquely different and bring different things to the table that, together, make us better. The moment you recognize someone else's gift, that really creates innovation, creativity, growth, and scalability. Everybody can work toward the good of the company mission with their own gifts. They're not just coming to the meeting, listening to your agenda, your next idea, or your next command that needs to be implemented. They're helping to build out your collective vision with you. That's the kind of culture people want to be a part of. That's when they feel part of something bigger.

Recap

This is all so much deeper than annual reviews (which I sure hope you're doing because if you aren't meeting them yearly to discuss their performance and give them a cost-of-living raise—at a minimum, you're missing the mark). Annual reviews should just be a summary of how we've loved you, cared for you, and served you—and—how you've served us, cared for our customers, improved, followed company policies, and gone above and beyond. It's about bringing together all the data and all the feedback and pointing it at one person. This allows both you and your employee to make any corrections along the way. There's a mutual affirmation that happens when you create a business where people want to stay.

True sticky culture goes much deeper, and building it requires intentionality, clear communication, and strategic actions that build loyalty, engage talent, and grow your organization. Culture is always evolving and it needs intentional effort and communication to grow with the business, rather than letting it evolve on its own. Building a good team culture happens when you can make sure the foundational elements of your business are good, starting with you. Then, sticky culture brings your people along with you.

We'll get into some practical applications for this in Part 3, but first, let's take a look at the last three pillars.

CHAPTER 7

SKILLED TECHNICIANS

Highly Valuable but Extremely Lacking

There's another component to the "people piece" of your business that, when done right, can have an amazing effect on the experience of your team. Taking this step has an equally amazing effect on the experience of your customers. The next pillar in the Leadership Playbook for the Trades is **Skilled Technicians**.

When your people are dialed in, your business becomes the one that customers *want* to work with because the people in your business become the kind of people *everyone* wants to work with. Your people are so important because they're the ones who actually make it all happen, you can't grow and scale sustainably without them.

But often, as I'm sure you are quite aware, the trades (and probably your business) are lacking in this area. To add to the problem, there's usually no specific plan to fix it by helping to train and grow our technicians. There may be developmental tasks, but since technicians are income generators, we often just ask if they have experience. If they say yes, we say, "Great, go ride in this guy's truck with him for two weeks and then get out there and make money." Then we wonder why they flood a house, have recalls, or why their sales aren't up. We also wonder why they leave us because someone else offered them $2 more per hour.

They don't stay when there's no growth plan to increase their skill, get training, certifications, or licensing, or where there's no strategic plan to move them up into the next technician level. We also miss the mark when it comes to creating clear paths to advance people into project manager or manager positions. When we don't talk about the big picture, we don't meet for reviews, and there's no mentorship, that's when we lose the people who could be our most valuable team members.

Training from the Beginning

Everyone knows there aren't a lot of people out there in the trades these days. We get applications from a kid just out of vo-tech school, a pizza delivery driver who's sick of delivering pizza and wants to be a plumber, or a landscaper who's tired of not having work in the winter. It's easy to reject all of them because they have no field experience and you have no feasible plan to develop and grow them into the trade.

So, to have skilled technicians, you need to develop them. You might need a plan for tiering based on skill level: apprentice, tech 1, tech 2, tech 3, and tech 4. You lay out what the differences are—what the pay scale looks like for each, what skills they need, and how many years they need to be in the trade before they can advance. Your techs probably already know their tier by the way they assign calls, the way you currently pay them, or the amount they get as a bonus, you just haven't formalized it yet. They're already doing this tiering mentally.

If you're going to hire the ex-pizza driver or the kid fresh out of vo-tech school, you'll need a well-defined mentorship program in place. This is a long road and should not be rushed. You'll need in-house training, on-the-road training with different departments, managers testing what they've learned, training in safety procedures, shift-differential practice, time for learning material, and practice at the crappiest job your company has to offer to ensure that they have enough grit to be a long-term employee.

When you lay it out on an organizational chart and groom your people into those tiers, you can hire and train team members more easily. And, when your people say they want to be a project manager or an estimator someday, you can say, "Great. Here are the steps."

Right now, if you are actually meeting with your techs (lots of owners in the trades don't), it's not usually about growth. It's usually just about sales—role-playing with them to push them to sell more and get a higher average ticket. But tradespeople don't want to be salesmen; they want to do the hands-on work of their trade. Meet your people where they are and offer them the paths to the skills that will help them and this will also help your company. Plus, when they have greater knowledge, they will be able to achieve upsells by sharing that additional information with customers.

Technician Growth

Employees want companies with growth potential and opportunity. To feel more invested in your company, they like to have a clear path to their own growth versus feeling like they're stuck in the same position for years without opportunities for them to advance. Whether it's through promotion or the development of new skills, people like to have the chance to grow and also move up in pay. The goal is to avoid a culture where employees feel like they're going to "die with a wrench in their hand" or be placed forever in the same role that is not of their choosing.

It's about creating a workplace where employees can explore and make choices about their career goals or find their special niche. They can see the steps clearly laid out in an organizational chart, know what they need to learn to reach their goals, or feel confident that they're already in the right spot for them.

This is why it is so helpful to create opportunities for your team to grow and take on more responsibilities. Some of the ways you can do that are the following:

- **Create tech levels and identify potential:** Establish technician ranking based on years in the trades, jobs they can handle, licenses and certifications that are needed, and pay scale ranges that apply to qualifications and soft skills required to move up in the rankings. Then begin to classify all your techs, identify your current leaders, your "up-and-comers," and those with potential. Start mentally plugging them into your future org chart and see how the departments in your organization can develop. Then, identify the training needed for those roles and specific people.

- **Establish a mentorship program for training:** Create a systematic, structured approach to move your techs through the levels created. This requires SOPs so that they know the correct way to do each job. You'll want to train them first with textbook and video training. (SkillCat is an excellent app for all trades; see the section in this book marked as Bonus Material for a free 30-day trial.) Then, you'll want to move them from in-house training in a safe environment to out-of-house training with supervision in the field. Finally, they can move up the ranks.

- **Training to overcome sales resistance:** Rather than role-playing or beating sales tactics over your technicians' heads, teach them strategies that close higher call tickets without crossing into the approach of a sleazy car salesman. This begins with product knowledge. Hold monthly meetings with vendors to teach your team the value of new products, how they work, how to fix them, and how to troubleshoot them in the field. This will give your techs more knowledge when facing tough customer questions. Another approach to teaching is with options pricing. This could be called Good-Better-Best or Silver-Gold-Platinum, whatever you want to call it. This helps your techs quote a minimum of three prices on each job—the bare minimum fix with the smallest warranty, the middle-of-the-road fix, and the best, most upgraded option with the longest warranty. This results in higher average call tickets and gives your techs the confidence they need to succeed.

If your people do decide it is time to learn more to move into a different role or take on different responsibilities, you can lay out the steps required for them to be able to gain those skills and move ahead. Help them get the technical skills they need to do the job they aspire to have.

How the "People" Pillars (Sticky Culture and Skilled Technicians) Work Together

On a day-to-day basis, make sure you're creating and hiring for the *culture* you want in your company. Then, make sure there are paths for training them with the needed *skills*. It's also important to have structured one-on-one check-ins with your people. So, how are you checking in with your management team? Your technicians?

You get a lot of information from meeting with a manager or team lead for about an hour to go over key topics that touch on culture *and* skill development. Ask them: What were the calls like? What's our backlog of work? Do we have any technician issues that need immediate attention? Any training that's required? What's the "real feel" (how are you really feeling in your job roles)?

Sometimes, the metrics and the "real feel" don't line up, and we want to know that so it's not a surprise later.

For our people, I break my teams into categories: executive team, managers, project managers by department, team leads, technicians, and apprentices. We also gather monthly with CSRs, dispatchers, the warehouse team, and marketing. It's important to collect feedback on where they are currently, where we're headed as a company, and what they think about some of our ideas. These are smaller, trusted groups that provide a lot of real, deep insight on a regular basis to know if any initiatives are actually helping us move forward. Then, we have buy-in from the top all the way down.

Recap

One of the byproducts of having these "people pieces" right (Sticky Culture and Skilled Technicians) is that word can get out. When your company is the one that is respectful of its employees, listens to and values them, and trains and develops them, people might just take notice. Then, when you place an ad to hire a tech, you'll likely stand a better chance at hiring someone who already has experience and better skills.

You'll know what brings them to your door. They heard about you. Somebody recommended you. They read good things in your ad. They hate where they're at. Those are the things that draw them to you. The best part is that when they get to you, you can truly look at cultural fit and you don't have to hire out of desperation. You'll keep your sticky culture and be able to hire and train more skilled technicians.

Through the pillar of Skilled Technicians, you'll develop training to keep your team growing and learning to better serve the business and your clients. They'll have a clear pathway for their career with you. When they see the path to becoming skilled technicians in a company that supports them, your people will be behind you all the way, and as you move forward, growth becomes almost unstoppable.

CHAPTER 8

EFFICIENT OPERATIONS

The Gears Behind Getting More Done

Nearly every time I'm coaching people, it is groundbreaking for them when they understand *how* they can delegate and *how* communication can happen. They learn how to process everything so that it all flows easily, from customer calls between the office and the technicians down to ordering and receiving material. When you fully understand the importance of efficiency and process, you and your team are going to get a whole lot more done, with a lot less effort!

The pillar of **Efficient Operations** helps provide this simplicity and understanding for you to build on as you move forward. Setting up your operations efficiently means you will know how people fit in your business, and as a result, you will have specific guidance for them.

So, if you've tried to hire, to move someone up to a new position in your organization, or to train your people, and none of your attempts have worked, it is not your fault. Other programs or coaches may have told you to implement some particular tool to change some aspect of the business, but if you don't lay out your operations, you'll lack the clarity that is required to understand what is needed—and you won't know when to implement the related actions. The pillar of Efficient Operations can help you set up the right structure so that what you need is clear.

Company Org Chart

If you're a small company, the first step to creating efficient operations might seem almost like overkill, but I promise, it's vital. You have to build an organizational chart and define the roles and responsibilities under each position. The reason to set up this structure is to see clearly where you are and define where you are going. The biggest mistake I see many owners in the trades make when first building their organizational chart is that they base it on exactly what they already have. Below is an example of an org chart given to me by someone I was working with the other day.

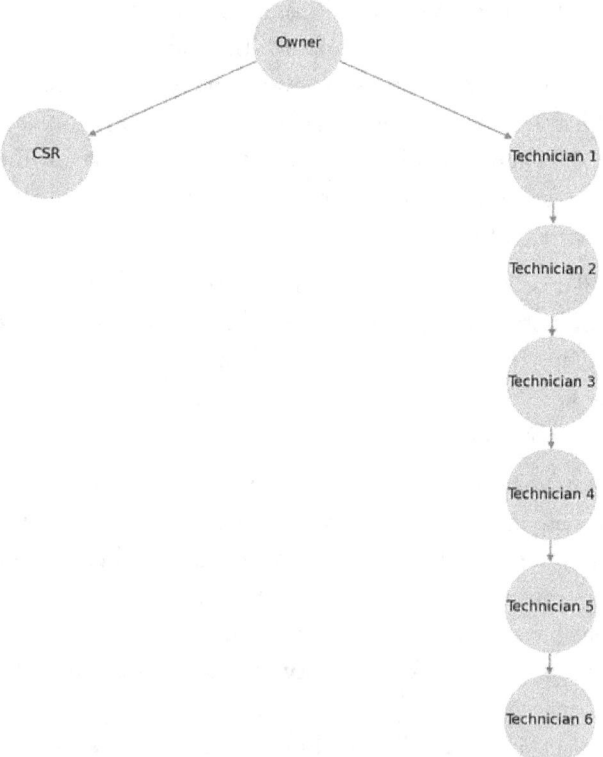

You can probably guess who fits where in the chart above—the owner at the top, one guy in charge of all seven techs, and a guy on the other side in charge of the office. But, this doesn't reflect where the company is going.

Where's marketing? Where's finance? Who's ordering materials? Is the service manager actually also the estimator, the trouble-shooter, the team lead, the trainer, and the warehouse guy? As you start listing these roles, you might realize that one person is handling them all. And that person is probably you, the owner. But other roles need to be represented on the chart, too (which will help immensely when it comes time to hire).

The correct way to build your organizational chart is horizontal, not vertical.

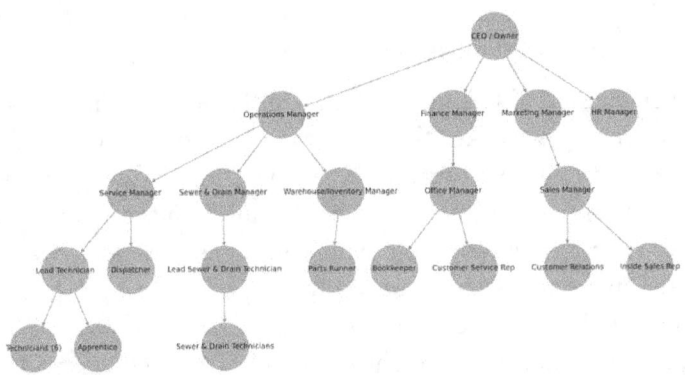

I want to encourage you to leave blanks on your org chart for the future positions you desire but that are not yet filled. No one should be on the organizational chart in multiple spots. If you're above a certain position and there's no one below you, you step down and fill that position until someone else can step in. My business partner, Luke, who brought so much of this org-chart wisdom to our company, often reminds our team that an organizational chart is not a place to say who's the most important: It's to show the level of responsibilities you have. As you move up the chart, you're not more important, your level of responsibilities just increases.

Brandon's First Aha

I worked with a guy named Brandon who is the head of the plumbing division at his company. He said that he didn't have enough time in his day to do all these "things," like creating an org chart, which is something you may be thinking right now. He kept saying that he had all these bottlenecks in his business, and fires to put out every single day. He didn't really know how to create space for himself to take more proactive approaches.

So, we started talking about what his dream organization might look like. Together, we listed it all out. He's the manager with a service manager under him, an estimator, and team leads. Then, we defined each of those individual roles.

When we started talking about the bottlenecks and fires he was experiencing, we talked through how all of those issues could be filtered through the organizational chart. He realized that very often, those bottlenecks weren't actually Brandon issues, they were team-lead issues, and the fires he was experiencing weren't Brandon problems, they were estimator problems. As he laid out responsibilities, Brandon also realized that he didn't need to lead *all* of the meetings. So now, he leads half of the meetings and the service manager leads the other half to handle service issues.

As they did for Brandon, these concepts become revolutionary for my clients. For the first time, they see how the whole business can operate more efficiently and create more time for them to think strategically.

Accountability

Maybe you're feeling the pressure of people, management, organization, and delegation. Maybe you already recognize that you need a service manager or an estimator position to handle some responsibilities. Then, just like Brandon, define what each position looks like, what it should accomplish, what burden the position is lifting, and what needs to be taken off your plate. Next, decide how to define each role, what responsibilities will be involved, etc.

When you break down your organizational chart, you identify which tasks and processes sit under which role so you can begin to create channels of communication and management protocols. You can then start to build accountability and know who to ask when something isn't done. After you set this up, no one will be able to say they didn't know it was their thing. Once the task is defined and assigned, the responsibility sits with them.

Standardization

Once you understand and have your roles and responsibilities laid out, you can create documentation for your key processes and describe how each role performs tasks and responsibilities. Processes for tasks such as customer onboarding, job scheduling, and service delivery need to be clarified so that you can standardize your operations and create consistency across the team. Here are some basic types of documentation that are essential in helping you set up these systems:

- **Standard Operating Procedures (SOPs):** We talked earlier about creating SOPs for skilled technicians, but we also need SOPs for all the processes in the office. This defines what is done for your company and how. These should be very detailed instructions for how to handle everyday tasks. Your SOPs could include instructions for how to interact with customers, how to complete jobs and job reporting, as well as how to follow regulations and safety protocols.

- **Employee Training Manuals:** In addition to learning SOPs, you want the new employees you're onboarding to be required to go through additional company materials outlining your specific company policies as well as standards for service and expectations for their specific roles.

- **Service Procedural Checklists**: Checklists, just like a grocery list, ensure that nothing is forgotten or missed. Having step-by-step instructions for technicians to follow helps them complete any service job according to company standards more efficiently. This keeps jobs more consistent between technicians so customers know what to expect.

- **Communication Pathway:** When you're bombarded every day about problems or things that aren't your responsibility, you tend to get bogged down. To fix this, get clear about the flow of communication—who communicates to whom, how communication should be done, and what steps are taken if things need to escalate. For example, if you set a process for technicians to contact the service manager first and they keep calling or texting you, kindly reply that they should reach out to their service manager. Then next time, don't answer, but let your service manager know so they can keep the chain of communication. This stops enabling people who don't follow the process. Stay consistent and you'll see the team begin to live into this, and it will *greatly* improve your efficiency.

One of the best places to begin to gather the information that you'll need in these documents is to, again, start with your team. Go to your people and ask them to write down what they do. Ask Sarah what it is that she actually does every day. Initially, she may say that she works in three departments and handles 35 different responsibilities—great. That's what you're documenting: each person's roles and how they do things. Plus, you're trying to understand a little better how you want things done so that you can lay out your systems correctly.

You want your people to do their jobs the same way, the right way, all the time. So, if you're moving someone out of a role and somebody's moving in, everything is documented for them to refer to as they go. If someone quits and that job's empty, you'll have a defined role and responsibilities *with* documentation, all so that you'll understand what the standardized process is for that role. This is a big help when you're trying to scale.

Creating standardization and documentation makes your processes all repeatable. Plus, standardization will put you in a better position to know which decisions to make and when to make them, such as who to hire next.

Recap

Look, at some point, things *will* go wrong, but you need to understand why things fall apart in the first place so that you can find ways to prevent the same issues from coming up again and again. Sometimes, you'll have to make adjustments or figure things out on the fly, but this can't be how you handle things every day. When you set up your efficient operations, everyone on your team understands their roles, their specific responsibilities, and their reporting structures.

You can get more shit done when you find enough balance for yourself to see where you need people within a structure that sets up the whole business for success. Once your business structures are in place, you'll want to know how everyone is doing. The next chapter will show you how to track if you've set your systems up correctly.

CHAPTER 9

CLEAR METRICS

The Illusion of Success

Business success can look dazzling from the outside—trucks rolling out, jobs being completed, and revenue charts climbing. But is that success real or is it an illusion? For many owners in the trades, success is measured solely by how much money is in the bank. But as I've seen time and time again, focusing on money alone will not build a strong foundation for growth. The pillar of **Clear Metrics** can help you look at this differently.

According to quoteinvestigator.com, in December 2005, Jim Carrey famously said to journalist Jay Stone of "The Ottawa Citizen" of Canada:

> "I think everybody should get rich and famous and [do] everything they ever dreamed of so they can see that that's not the answer."

Early in his acting career, even Jim Carrey found that chasing bigger and bigger accomplishments often led to emotional disappointment, prompting his comment about wealth and fame not being the ultimate answer. Material success does not necessarily equate to personal fulfillment.

Money can't be the *only* metric you drive at or you'll push until you burn yourself and your people out. You, your culture, and ultimately your business will suffer. Success needs to be guided by humility, fueled by accountability, and sustained by service. You'll need to confront hard truths about your business and find ways to scale that serve not just your wallet, but also your people and your purpose.

It is said that the love of money is the root of all evil, and in order to break free from the illusion that money alone equals success, you need a framework that grounds you in reality. You need the pillar of Clear Metrics to provide you with a continuous feedback loop—to gather data, reflect on it, and make intentional decisions. Even if you are a healthy owner and have clearly laid out your efficient operations, if you don't get some true data, you won't know what's *actually* happening in your business. This means that any decision you make will only be a guess—and guessing has a much lower rate of success. Clear metrics take out the guesswork.

So, in this chapter, we'll look at different kinds of metrics and how to define what's important. Here's how clear metrics work:

1. **Collect Data**: Track the metrics that matter most, based on your specific business and personal goals. These could include profit and loss, a specific dollar amount on each service call, employee satisfaction, or customer feedback, just to name a few.

2. **Analyze**: Use questions to help you identify the gaps. What's working? What's not? What does the data show? You'll also gather information and insights from your team, which might challenge your assumptions, but will also give you a clearer picture. This feedback will help you understand the numbers better.

3. **Take Action**: What changes need to be implemented based on the data and feedback? Adjust the processes, create

additional training, or reallocate resources as needed to improve specific outcomes.

4. **Reflect**: Track the changes you've made. Did they have the desired effect? What results do you see now? Use those outcomes to refine your approach and continue to make changes as needed by going back to the top and collecting data again.

The point of clear metrics is that this feedback loop is never-ending. Success isn't a destination; it's a process of continuous improvement. You'll use the data you find to connect the dots. Metrics always tell the truth about where you are and where you're headed. They'll also help you make real-time decisions and create best practices for your business.

Clear metrics are designed to keep your business aligned with your goals even as those goals change. When you define what's most important first, you can establish your strategic goals and identify the metrics you'll use as indicators or milestones for those goals. You'll create metrics for yourself (see the Balance Wheel and Alignment Assessment in Part 3, which you can track over time), you'll create metrics for others to use for feedback and training, and you'll create metrics for the business so that your team can assess performance and plan for future demands.

The Courage to See Clearly and Be Accountable

For many owners, looking at these clear metrics might feel threatening. But knowing the truth isn't a weakness, it's a strength. As a leader, you have to model this accountability—own your mistakes, follow through on your commitments, and be the first to embrace change.

It takes incredible courage to look clearly at your metrics, to admit when something isn't working, and most importantly, to do the hard work of fixing whatever is broken. The real power of clear metrics lies in turning what you learn into action. It's about setting clear goals, tracking progress, and holding yourself and your team accountable for outcomes.

Clear metrics have multiple functions based on what matters to your business. For example, if you want your average call ticket to be $500, obviously, you would monitor the key metric of your average call ticket. But there are other metrics that could indicate why you are or are not hitting that $500. Are these jobs residential or commercial calls? Is your pricing in line? Are your techs upselling and offering multiple pricing options?

When you look deeper into the metrics, maybe you find that you've only been doing small, residential jobs with low invoice totals. This could be a problem that requires your marketing to be adjusted, a technician skill issue that requires training, or a procedural change for how your technicians show confidence in front of customers or how they upsell. We want to understand the main metric that shows us the win or loss, but we also need the courage to go deeper to find that metric.

Leading and Lagging Metrics

Leading and lagging metrics will often give you information that allows you to go deeper into what you are tracking. You might be most familiar with lagging metrics, which tell you what has already been done. These are your records for job completion, revenue, profit, etc. Hopefully, you are already using reports based on lagging metrics to find ways to do things better next time.

Other metrics are leading and show what hasn't been done yet and might be able to forecast if there's a problem coming. Leading metrics often show numbers that let you know what's on the horizon. They see the forecast of work and cash flow. They see how customer issues might be resolved before they become complaints because your people can take action before there's a bigger problem.

For example, if three customers haven't been called back and three estimates haven't been scheduled, that's not necessarily a problem—yet. But it will be a problem if you don't take action to complete those tasks. The metrics look at the key things—the things that make the business run, that make it sustainable, that provide the customer service, and that you have written into your mission, vision, and values. Plus, these metrics will help you ensure that you're doing those things and doing them well.

I'm always blown away by the leading metrics—they may be concerning or exciting, but they're always very accurate. At one of our metrics meetings, my finance guy looked over to my finance manager and said that cash flow was going to be really difficult for the next four weeks—before it happened. The cash flow at that moment was perfectly fine, but because of the clear metrics, he could see the money coming in, the jobs being sold, and knew we needed to prepare for a $225,000 dip.

Do you know what your cash flow looks like in the next 30 days? What caused your last dip, and how can you prevent that next time? Knowing these answers by using the proper metrics will change your business for the better!

Clear metrics help us spot trends. For example, we might realize we need to push harder in August because September tends to slow down. When we know that in advance, we can plan for it the following year. We need to strategize so that we don't have cash flow dips or people sitting around in September. We can plan for training or decide not to get every job done in August. Maybe you discount jobs for people who will wait, so you can schedule them in September because you'll need the work then. There's so much value in these clear, leading metrics.

Metrics tell how much solid work there is, how many quotes are out, how many dispatches are opened, etc. When you do the math, you can identify trends to see whether you're averaging out, falling behind, or running high. Because if we keep trending high, guess what? We're hiring. If we keep trending low, we better fix marketing or sales to get that back up or we're going to dip again. Having these leading and lagging metrics really helps people understand and plan for future workload fluctuations.

More Metrics

Clear metrics also help track the standardization of your operational efficiency. For example, if you expect estimates to be sent within seven days of being created, track a metric indicating what day an estimate was created and have it notify you on day seven if the estimate hasn't been sent. That's when you'll know what's actually getting done.

You can also build company and financial dashboards made up of charts, graphs, and other visual representations of your business's important metrics and KPIs. This will allow you to see at a glance how the company is doing.

But, you'll also create metrics specifically around job roles and responsibilities. You'll have a dashboard for your customer service rep (CSR), for example, with lots of customization that applies directly to her job roles and responsibilities. She might see that the company as a whole is doing well, but that doesn't necessarily mean she's doing her job successfully. The CSR dashboard will show you if she's meeting her metrics and doing her job well.

So, we have dashboards for our CSRs, our technicians, our project managers, and our dispatchers. Every department has a dashboard of metrics that applies specifically to what they do. That's how we use core metrics. And that's why the org chart has to be built, why roles have to be put in place, why responsibilities have to be assigned, and why technology has to function.

These metrics also give a more accurate temperature on the business. I have seen lots of people, lots and lots of people, think they're doing great when in reality the business is performing terribly. That's because being busy is not success. People recognizing their value and living into their responsibilities while hitting the goals of their metrics is true success.

Defining What's Important

Clear metrics can only work for you if you know how to use them. You could put every number and every metric you want up on your wall. You can quickly overwhelm yourself with numbers. But don't let the data drown you. Irrelevant numbers that won't help you hit your goals will have you chasing aimlessly and will burn you out. The only thing you need to know is what you're trying to achieve, and then track the metric that tells you how well you're doing that.

Let's say you want to lose weight and gain muscle. Great! You will definitely want a metric for your weight and BMI to track your main goals. But you might also want metrics for how many workouts you do or what your protein intake is because those also help you work toward your goal. You don't need to know the temperature in the gym, when the weights were replaced, or the gym membership numbers.

You don't want to focus on the wrong things, or irrelevant information, so you should decide what will help you accomplish *your* goals specifically. This is where the hard work of defining what matters comes in. Then, you can take your data and craft beautiful dashboards that represent what's most important— these metrics report the right things. The metrics may be just numbers, charts, and graphs, but the right ones can show you the truth of your business when you understand how they relate to your goals.

Once you define what's important for you as a healthy owner and for your efficient operations, clear metrics are what help make those plans a reality. To determine the right metrics to look at, you have to go back to your strategic plan. Answer the big questions and write out your goals. From there, you can define your key action steps, which are what you're actually going to do to accomplish your goal.

Recap

Only clear metrics can help you truly understand the health of your business. Without defining and tracking your important KPIs, you're basing decisions on whims or emotions. Metrics remove emotions. They aren't swayed by the highs and lows; they just report the facts. And, when you can balance emotions with facts, you'll have a dynamic moving force in your business.

By deciding what is most important for you and your business first, you'll be able to see clearly what data you need to focus on. Then, you can track that data through the systems and processes you have set up and be able to make better decisions.

Tracking clear metrics also helps you set goals that are realistic and well-defined. You won't lose sight of the progress you are making to grow your business, and you won't miss opportunities for improvement or optimization. You'll see trends as they are coming through leading information and be able to better assess alternatives to handle or capitalize on them.

Each time you approach the feedback and the review of your metrics, it will help to approach them with humbleness and a willingness to learn. The numbers are just information, they're not judgments. They can show you what is working well and what needs more work. Tracking the true metrics, the real data, and applying what you learn to the decisions you are making will help you reach your long-term, strategic goals so much sooner than you ever thought possible.

This isn't easy work. It will challenge you, frustrate you, and push you to grow. But on the other side of it is something far more valuable than money: fulfillment, legacy, and the peace of mind that comes from knowing you've built something that truly matters.

Part 3 will go into the practical steps to get you started on your journey to the other side. You've mastered your trade, now you can master the *business* of your trade as well and turn the illusion of success into real success. Let's start applying the playbook so you can see and feel what a difference it can make!

PART 3
Applying the Playbook

CHAPTER 10

WHERE TO START

Beginning the Leadership Playbook for the Trades is like building a strong foundation for your business—you'll create a solid base to build it on.

As we've walked through the playbook, you've learned the steps to build the systems and processes that will help you weather the changes and fluctuations that you know are coming. This is where the slow growth comes in. It's not about ramping up super fast and burning out. It's about creating a sustainable business that grows, even as you endure the ups and downs.

Slow and Steady

I'll be honest, the speed at which you see results depends on you and your specific situation. This is not a quick fix—it's not about trying to make everything perfect in a short amount of time. Some things *will* happen fast. You might have some immediate breakthroughs in how you handle cash flow, or you may hire your first technician and feel the relief of not doing everything yourself.

But the *real* transformation comes in the long term—after six months, a year, or even more time has passed. This framework is built for sustainable success, which means you might not see explosive growth right away, but you'll see incremental, steady improvements. And those improvements, compounded over time, are what will allow you to scale confidently and sustainably.

At the end of the day, you will have a business that can survive turnover, seasonality, debt, and all the challenges that come with being in the trades. You'll also be able to make better decisions because you won't be flying by the seat of your pants anymore. You'll have the playbook as a guide to get you through. But you have to be willing to put in the work, make the decisions, and trust the process. If you do that, you'll be able to face the fluctuations and the stress with much more confidence.

Role of the Playbook

The Leadership Playbook for the Trades will give you a sense of control and direction in a world where, without this specific structure, it's easy to feel like you're just reacting to everything— constantly putting out fires. And as much as you're still going to face the grind, the pressure, and all those other realities, you at least have a way to manage them. You know that you're doing the right things at the right time, and that you're building something that will grow with you, not against you.

So, even when things are tough, you won't feel like you're crazy or like you're drowning. You'll know where you're headed and that you're on the path to creating not just a successful business, but a sustainable one. It's about building the habits, systems, and mindset that allow you to weather those inevitable storms and keep your eyes on your bigger goals.

Peace doesn't mean everything's easy or that all your problems will disappear. There's no magic fix; it's about managing the inevitable chaos with purpose. It's having a framework that allows you to look at your challenges and know exactly what to do about them. And then, slowly, you'll start seeing results— whether that's more revenue, better retention, or even just time to step away for a well-earned break.

This isn't just about surviving anymore; it's about thriving with more clarity, confidence, and peace of mind. Whether you're running a two-person shop or scaling to a larger team, this framework keeps bringing you back to the fundamentals—the foundation that makes everything else possible. The work never stops, but with the right approach, it becomes manageable, purposeful, and ultimately rewarding.

Peace comes from knowing you're not alone in this—knowing you have a playbook. When you get started with this, you won't just be reacting to what comes your way. You'll be able to actively drive your business forward, and that's a powerful feeling.

Quick Wins

In the next two chapters, we're going to dive in and deliver some quick wins to get you started on your path to a more peaceful, more profitable business. You'll notice that only the first two pillars are covered in this section—Healthy Owner and Sticky Culture. This is because I'm here to help you, not overwhelm you. It's just not possible to cover every part of all of the pillars in one little book. You would probably throw your hands up, feeling inundated—and you've experienced enough of that already. I'm not trying to add to that.

To dig into the playbook, you have to own your crap and help your people *first*. Because when I coach an owner, I can't talk about clear metrics (or SOPs, training programs, etc.) without first talking about being a healthy owner.

I've chosen these quick wins because you can implement them right now. Once you get your mindset and leadership right, and you get your culture right (nice and sticky), things will flow so much better. For everything else, you can dig into the Bonus Material at the end of the book.

You have all of the information you need in this book, but drilling down in these two pillars will set you up to care for your two *greatest* assets...you and your people. Once you are on the right path, you can take on more information in the Bonus Material to take your company even further. When you go through this additional material, you'll find additional resources for the other three pillars, including a template for a one-page strategic plan, a 30-day free trial to SkillCat technician training, tools for hiring technicians, a spreadsheet for clear metrics, and more. Be sure to check out these valuable tools to use in your business.

But first, let's dig in and get you some quick wins!

CHAPTER 11

BECOME A
HEALTHY OWNER

The Leadership Playbook for the Trades starts with you. This might be the most difficult part of the process, but it's essential to understand this pillar before you can build on any of the other pillars.

We talked about what it looks like to be a healthy owner in Chapter 5 when we discussed the five things needed for a peaceful business: embrace humility; hire smarter; raise up leaders; have the heart of a servant; and know your mission, vision, and values.

This part might not be easy. You'll have to commit to being humble and ready to learn. To get the most out of this pillar, it helps to be hungry for something better, both at home and at work. It's going to take work on your part to get the changes the Leadership Playbook for the Trades promises. Are you ready?

Let's start with the first step. When I'm working directly with an owner or speaking to a room full of owners, we start with the balance wheel below.

LIFE & LEADERSHIP
BALANCE WHEEL

Think Through:

Whats most important to you?

What does a 10 mean? Perfect or to much focus?

What does a balanced life look like?

Is it possible to do it all & run a business?

Big Wins & Big Losses in Past Month

I'll ask you, just like I ask them, to take 15 minutes and fill out the balance wheel. You'll see that the numbers 1 to 10 go out from the spokes around the wheel. Take a look at each of the categories and place a mark on the wheel where you are on this scale. Base the number on your current level of satisfaction—with 1 being the worst and 10 being the best. For example, if you are feeling secure and fulfilled in your family, you might rate it at an 8 or 9. If you don't have a supportive community, you might rate that area at a 2 or 3. Do this assessment with honesty and humility, but don't overthink this. Just make a note of where you are on the wheel in each of the categories.

Once you have completed the balance wheel, it's time to take a look at the 5-point alignment assessment.

5-POINT ALIGNMENT ASSESSMENT

	Behind Target	On Target	Ahead of Target
Revenue Generation Sales, marketing, dispatches, average invoice total, truck per hour and customer relationships	O	O	O
Operations Management Material supply chain, inventory control, technology, and administration	O	O	O
Organizational Development Recruitment, right people right seat, talent development, talent management, and succession	O	O	O
Financial Management Goals, projections, metrics, controls, reporting, and cash management	O	O	O
Giving Back Culture & Community impact, Giving & serving your employees and neighbors through your business	O	O	O

Rate yourself on these categories, whether you are behind target, on target, or ahead of target. Once you have completed this second assessment, really contemplate where you fall on both of these to determine your current balance and alignment.

Really take some time to sit with the information you get from these. Do your results surprise you or did you know how close or how far off the mark you were? Does anything come immediately to mind for things you could do to get more balance and alignment?

What the Assessments Mean

At a recent speaking engagement, I had people fill out these two assessments, just like you did. When everyone was done, I asked the room of over 150 people, "How many of you are happy with how your balance wheel looks?" Nobody raised their hands. Then I asked, "How many of you are ahead in all five categories of your business alignment?" Still, no hands went up.

That reminded me why I have owners use these assessments. Here we are, sacrificing everything we love and value, grinding it out, thinking, "If I just sacrifice more here, I'll get ahead in these other areas of the business." But in this room of over 150 people, not one person was ahead.

The point is, you're working your ass off, sacrificing your balance wheel to make your business amazing, but when you put it on paper, your business *isn't* amazing and your life isn't either. This means that what you're doing is broken. You are compromising too much, and it's not getting results.

To address this, you'll need to define your long-term vision by reflecting on your personal values and goals. Write down a vision for where you want to be in five to 10 years. It's also helpful to write down what you want others to say about you, or what you've accomplished, when you are gone. Then, ensure this vision aligns with your business goals and personal life priorities. Let's find out how these assessments can help you become a healthy owner.

Prioritize Physical and Emotional Health

Most people in the trades don't exactly practice self-care on a regular basis, but being an owner with a healthy and balanced life is the foundation for becoming a truly effective leader. This doesn't have to mean taking bubble baths, but making your physical and emotional stability a priority allows you to show up as your best self at work and at home. There will be many, many highs and lows with business ownership and being able to navigate that with clarity and resilience will be life-changing. No more barking orders and later having regrets (with your kids, your spouse, *or* your team).

The Balance Wheel above provides a way to assess, and therefore improve, each of the key areas of life. It helps you find a balance between your business, with all it requires of you, and your personal life. Let's take a look at how each of the categories in the balance wheel connect with your physical and emotional health.

Keys to Use the Balance Wheel

On your completed Balance Wheel, you'll have a framework showing a clear picture of where you may be out of balance in the eight key areas. The ratings you now have will guide you on where to focus to make intentional improvements. Below are some ideas to address that have the potential to improve scores in each area. It's time to create a life that is so much more fulfilling.

1. **Marriage and Family**: This is more valuable and important than your business. Culture begins at home. To make strides in this category, find ways to dedicate time and energy to building and nurturing your relationships. Plan a dinner out, see a movie with the kids, take a weekend away to connect,

visit your parents. Make sure these activities get added to your calendar and then marked off completed.

2. **Support Community**: Can you name a friend you can trust with anything? Someone who'd be there for you, hold your darkest secrets, and celebrate your greatest wins without getting emotionally rattled? If you can't, it's time to get one. Build a community that includes like-minded individuals, coaches, mentors, and friends. Find groups in your personal and professional life. Connect with a church group, meet your neighbors, coach your kid's sports team, or volunteer with an organization that's meaningful to you. Maybe you'll meet someone you can build a support system with.

3. **Personal Finance**: Do you know how much you have in savings and investments? How much do you need to retire? Do you have any financial goals like sending your kids to college, paying for your daughter's dream wedding, traveling the world, or buying a vacation home? Develop a budget with a spending and savings plan for your personal finances and keep those separate from your business finances. This ensures you're not putting your personal security on the line for your business. I highly recommend you find a financial advisor— sit down with them, share your dreams, and develop a plan to get there.

4. **Fitness and Nutrition**: How's your health? Your cholesterol? Are you at your goal weight? How many times a week are you eating fast food? I recommend you schedule regular physical activity in your calendar first thing in the morning before going straight into the office. You can establish a daily routine that includes exercise, healthy eating, and mindfulness practices. Do fun activities and try healthy new recipes to stay motivated.

5. **Fun and Recreation**: Honestly, when was the last time you had fun or went on a vacation without doing any work? Set

a time each month to pursue your favorite hobbies, spend some time in nature, or socialize with your friends. God did not create life to be just work. The to-do list will never end, but your sanity might if you don't find a way to take a break.

6. **Leading Others**: If you're reading this book, you are a leader in one way or another, but are you leading by example? Recognize you're a leader and that others are watching. Would others want to follow the life you are leading? It's hard to lead people to places you haven't been to yourself. Read books (after this one, of course) on habits, leadership, and communication styles to sharpen your skills.

7. **Emotional Stability**: How do you react to stress or annoying situations? When driving, does your middle finger get more exercise than the other four? Maybe it's time to find ways to become more self-aware. Take time to step back and see what emotions you felt (and showed) during different situations as they arise. Consider a personality test like Enneagram to understand yourself better. And, don't be afraid to get a counselor or a coach. There's no shame in talking with someone about what you've been through in life—it's had an impact. For me, some deep breaths, a prayer for wisdom and peace, a reminder that God's got me, and learning to be ok with the fact that some things are out of my control really help.

8. **Rest and Retreat**: How many hours are you sleeping at night? How well are you sleeping? Sleep is important and if you're constantly working and worrying, you're most likely lacking. Don't fight it. Make sleep a priority. For retreat, I'm talking about taking the time to sit on a beach, on a mountaintop, or in a park without your phone or any distractions—time to just think and contemplate your life, your goals, wins, and failures. A time when you actually give yourself some space.

Can you sit still without your phone? Do you know what silence with no distractions feels like? I recommend that you schedule at least two days per year. You might find this practice of retreat to be life-changing.

From the information you got by filling out the Balance Wheel, concentrate your focus on the areas with lower scores and try some of these action steps to help improve them. For example, if your fitness score is low, set a strategic goal for regular exercise. If your marriage and family score is low, get out your calendar and start by finding a day to connect with your family over a meal or a shared activity and then make that a part of your ongoing schedule. If the area of personal finance needs work, make budgeting a priority or schedule that meeting with a financial advisor.

You don't have to set goals for each of your low-scoring categories all at once. Choose one or two areas that you can focus on each month. I recommend starting with your lower scores and making small and consistent efforts in those targeted areas. Gradually, you will build a life that is more balanced and resilient.

Define Your Long-Term Vision

Now that you have a good idea of where you sit on the Balance Wheel, defining your long-term vision will help you identify and define what truly matters to you so that you can create a life that is a reflection of your priorities. Having a vision that is both clear and meaningful goes way beyond just business success—this is an encapsulation of your values and your personal dreams. This is the stuff that legacy is built on. By making the time to create and articulate your vision, you will gain a clear, renewed direction for your life. Your vision will also provide powerful support and motivation when you are met with challenges.

Crafting a Vision Statement

Your personal vision statement is a unique roadmap that captures your deepest goals and aspirations in life. This vision provides clarity on how you wish to be remembered when you are gone and what impact you hope to leave—for your family, community, and business. Here are some key questions that will help you explore as you craft your own vision statement.

- **Defining Your Vision:**
  - » What do you truly wish to do? Where do you want to be in the next five years—in your life and business?
  - » What motivates and drives you—both personally and professionally?
  - » If you have previously written a personal vision statement, does it deeply resonate with what you hold as most valuable in life? If not, which key elements are missing?
  - » Plan to revisit your vision statement at least annually (quarterly is even better in the early stages) to ensure that it still aligns with your evolving priorities.

- **Values and Priorities:**
  - » What are your top values, and how do they influence the way you make decisions in your personal and professional life?
  - » What do you hope people remember most about you when you are no longer here? List the top three qualities that you want to have associated with you.
  - » Does your current lifestyle reflect the legacy you hope to leave? If not, what changes could you make to be in better alignment?

- **Reflection on Legacy:**
  - » What qualities, achievements, and/or contributions would you want to have highlighted when people speak about you?

>> If someone were to read a eulogy for you today, what would you want said about your impact and your character?
>> What actions or behaviors do you consider essential components to build the legacy you desire?
>> Are there small, daily actions that you can build on?

Steps to Bring Your Vision to Life

The first step to bringing your vision to life is to get out a piece of paper or a notebook and actually write it all down. Having such an important statement on paper makes it much more tangible, and it serves as a reminder of your long-term goals.

Another key piece of living your vision statement is to review it on a regular basis. It is great to set some time aside each month or each quarter to review and make any adjustments to your vision as needed. This will help you make sure that it continues to reflect your priorities as you and your business evolve.

The final step to bringing your vision to life is to use it as a decision-making guide. When you face a major decision in life or in business, pull out your vision statement and use it to help guide you in any course of action. Your choices should always align with your long-term goals so that you are building the life and legacy that you intend.

Defining your personal long-term vision provides a clear path for you toward a more fulfilling life. It also provides both motivation and direction as you continue on your journey as a business owner.

Sample Vision Statements

Below are some sample vision statements that can help you see how the concepts we just discussed might be used to create one of these statements. I hope these examples can inspire you to think of what might be possible for you as well.

"I am a supportive leader who fosters a culture of collaboration, empathy, and growth. My mission is to build a successful business that exceeds the needs of our customers and also creates opportunities for personal and professional development for my team. I am committed to achieving financial success while building strong relationships with my family, my community, and my team. I want to leave a legacy of kindness and positive impact with everyone I meet."

"My vision is to lead with integrity, building a business that enhances people's lives and fosters growth. I seek to inspire others through authentic connections. I embrace change and aim to leave a legacy of meaningful impact in both my business and personal life."

"My vision is to be a catalyst for positive change—in business and in life. I believe that success is built on connections, empathy, and a commitment to lifelong learning. I strive to build a business that not only generates profit but also nurtures the well-being of those it reaches. By creating an environment of innovation, respect, and personal growth, I will actively live a life that is both successful and meaningful. My legacy rises beyond traditional measures of success."

Now it's your turn. Go through the steps and questions above and jot down some notes to craft your own vision statement. It doesn't have to be perfect, but getting this information together can give you a great place to start.

Creating a Strategic Plan

Once you know your long-term vision, the next step is creating a strategic plan that outlines how you'll take the steps to get you there. By understanding what matters most to you, you can set specific, measurable goals that align with your vision. This will help your daily actions move you closer to your goals and aspirations. This plan is not only a guide for growth, it is also a tool to help you keep focused—so you can prioritize what truly matters and can avoid distractions.

Your Strategic Plan

The strategic plan takes the priorities and goals that you have identified and then turns them into specific and achievable steps that can help you build toward your vision. This way, you will have a roadmap so that you are always moving in the direction you want to go.

1. Start by taking a closer look at your vision statement to identify what the core priorities are that will drive your life and your business forward. Choose the top three to five areas that are the most important to you, and list them out. Once you list these priorities, you will have a foundation for setting goals that are more meaningful to you because they will be based on your highest values.

2. Next, with this list of three to five priorities, take a look at your day, week, and month. Identify if there are any things that you spend time on that are in direct conflict with reaching your goals. Then think about how you can find ways to make changes so that you can keep your focus on what matters most to you.

3. Once you have removed the items that are in direct conflict with your goals, the next step will be to create one or two short-term actions that you can do weekly, monthly, or quarterly. So, for a financial example, you could save a percentage of your income to invest in your long-term financial goal and you could plan for quarterly reviews of your investments to make adjustments as needed.

4. Finally, it is critically important to schedule time for regular check-ins on these goals to gauge where you are. You will

want to assess any progress made for each goal, celebrate any wins towards those goals, and make any adjustments to keep moving forward toward your ultimate vision. Taking this time to celebrate and adjust keeps you motivated as you move forward.

Setting Boundaries

An essential part of being able to achieve your vision is learning when to say "no" to anything that isn't in alignment with your priorities. This might mean having to decline certain business opportunities. It could also mean delegating certain tasks, or setting strict boundaries around your time.

You will have to learn to evaluate any new opportunities by asking yourself if they align with your current vision and priorities *before* you commit to taking on new projects or ventures. If the actions in question don't align, saying yes to them may take you further from your ultimate goals.

Setting boundaries will also mean protecting your time. You will need to delegate to your team and empower them to be able to handle the tasks that don't actually require your direct involvement. This allows you to be able to focus on the activities that will have a higher impact toward achieving your goals, while protecting your personal time. It's important to schedule your personal and family time in the same way you would for work commitments—honor and make these times non-negotiable.

Creating a strategic plan and building boundaries around it will allow you to build a life that is centered on what truly matters to you—so that both your personal and business life align with your vision.

At the end of each month, take a look at how you spent your time to see if there are things you could have handled differently to have stayed in better alignment. Your strategic plan is there to keep you focused, motivated, and confident that each step you are taking will lead you closer to the future of your dreams.

Recap

Prioritizing your personal well-being and what matters most to you will help you build a stable foundation for success. By maintaining balance across these areas, you create emotional stability and resilience, which in turn strengthens your leadership and prepares you for the ongoing demands of business ownership. A healthy owner can also inspire a healthy team. And, working together with your team, you will be able to create a workplace that can support sustainable long-term growth. When you make consistent investments in your well-being, you fuel your business's success today *and* build a foundation that will ensure that your legacy endures.

CHAPTER 12

CREATE A STICKY CULTURE

Let's take a deeper look at this pillar of Sticky Culture. We'll explore the best way for your team to function as you work with them to build something you can grow. Remember, sticky culture creates the kind of company where people want to stay. So, let's take a look at the first steps under this pillar, which are to define your core values and then establish how you're going to start talking to the people on your team consistently.

Define Core Values for Your Business

Core values lead the way as you develop how you want your business and the people in it to behave. When these values are clearly communicated and consistently reinforced, they create alignment among your team. And when values give you and your team members purpose, they encourage the kind of behaviors that can contribute to a more positive work environment, which also leads to higher customer satisfaction.

The process here is similar to what you did in the Healthy Owner pillar when you asked yourself what you want others to say about you when you're gone. Here, you're coming back to your values and connecting them to your long-term vision to ask, "What is important to us as a company? What defines us and will ultimately help us become who we want to be as a business? What do we want to represent when our business is gone, or we're gone from our business?" Looking deeply into those questions really helps to define your business. In discussions around these questions, it's best to include your top leaders, key people, innovators, different generations, etc. You want them all to sit in on this process and be part of it with you.

Find Your Core Values

Collaboration with your team is the best way to establish meaningful values for your company. Employees also feel more connected to these values from the beginning when they are included in the process of creating them, which strengthens their commitment to upholding them. Why? Because these are the values that should reflect the behaviors and principles that guide your whole company.

One way you can create a collaborative environment is by conducting a core-values workshop where everyone comes together. Below are the steps to run such a workshop.

1. **Set the Groundwork**: It's best to start by explaining how important core values are and how they can impact the business, as well as the dynamics of the team. Discuss the benefits of having these values defined—team cohesion, better decisions, and enhanced customer service.

2. **Brainstorm**: Ask each team member to consider qualities that they believe are essential for both personal and business success so that they can share them with you and the team. Examples of these qualities might include quality, integrity, respect, or teamwork.

3. **Narrow the List**: Review the key values the team came up with and group together ideas that are similar. After that, identify the top five values that resonate most with those on

the team, yourself included. These are the values to prioritize so that you can all reflect the company's vision and goals in your actions.

4. **Define the Values**: For each value, define it in practical terms by creating a short definition along with examples of behaviors that embody it. This can help clarify how each team member can demonstrate the core values in their work on a daily basis.

Here are some examples.

- One value might be integrity, which could be defined as, "We commit to being honest and ethical and doing what's right even when no one is watching."

- Another could be customer focus, which can be explained by saying, "We prioritize customer needs by providing reliable, quality service to exceed the expectations of those we serve."

- A focus on continuous improvement might include something like, "We embrace learning and growth. We are always looking to improve skills, processes, and the customer's experience."

Bring Your Core Values to Life

Once you have your core values, it's essential that they are visible to the team as they should be easily integrated into daily operations. Steps to ensure that these core values become a part of the company culture include displaying them prominently, including them in discussions during onboarding, and making sure they are used in meetings to do a cultural "refresh."

Your core values should be posted in locations that are visible within your workplace. Places like the break room or the main office are good for this. You can also include them on your website or in company materials, both internal and customer-facing. And new hires should be introduced to these values from day one. This ensures that expectations for behavior and performance are set early. Plus, this will also help you make sure each new hire is a good fit in the company culture.

Quarterly check-in meetings will allow the team to reflect on how well the values are being upheld. These meetings will also allow your team to have open feedback, receive recognition for embodying the company values, and offer suggestions if adjustments should be made.

When core values for your business are clearly defined and consistently reinforced, they create a shared identity that deeply strengthens the company's culture. Employees who are able to understand and live by these core values contribute to a more cohesive and purpose-driven workplace where everyone feels like they are on the same team.

Employee Engagement

After you and your team have decided on the core values that your company will live into, it's time to start building out how you're going to keep talking to your people. You should have one-on-one meetings, feedback surveys, and team meetings that include trust building because these efforts are where the heartbeat of your company is. And, the more you know about your company's heartbeat, the better you will be able to lead. That's the simplicity of it. Establishing these engagement structures is pretty much just a fancy way of saying ... get out your dang calendar and block off some time.

An example from my own company is a man who's been in plumbing for over 30 years. He is currently working his way up to be a plumbing manager in our company. Recently, he said that he is really looking forward to doing one-on-one meetings with technicians as part of his new role, because that wasn't how he handled things in the past. He got excited about this role from seeing how other leaders in the company work. Everybody knows he's the best and has tons of experience. He has definitely proven himself. Now, he's over 50, and it's time for him to start working towards what the next 10 to 15 years of his career will look like—and that can't be upside down under a sink.

In our company, we've encouraged this kind of engagement several times, and it's fun that I'm no longer the one leading the charge. Our CSO, who taught me plumbing and has been with the company 32 years, is now the one bringing this guy up to speed and moving him into the role of plumbing manager. We work to make sure these kinds of opportunities are baked into our culture. I'm not just making this up, we actually *do* this stuff, and I've seen how well these strategies work firsthand.

Now, if you're new to this, it can be a different experience when you sit down and actually commit to talking to your people in meetings or one-on-one. It's a little extra work and you might have some fear about what individuals might bring up. Maybe one of your guys has a massive home problem. Maybe he's not really a dick, maybe his wife is sick and that affects him at work. But, if you don't create the time for relationships, you're never going to know those things. And then you're gonna have poor feedback from the customers that person is serving because you don't know the depth of what that team member is going through, which means you can't address it to offer them the proper support.

Create Employee Engagement

There are several ways to establish this type of employee engagement. There are ways that you can have fun and stay connected within your company. So, what do you do as a whole company to create camaraderie? Do you have a picnic or Christmas party? How about for your road warriors (the techs that are out on job sites every day)? Do you create time for them to come back to the shop and connect with the team? Team building creates deep roots for a strong and healthy culture. You can build that time together by making time to have meetings both with the team as well as one-on-one.

Team Meetings

One effective way to build engagement is through a structured, monthly team meeting. The structure of this meeting is designed specifically to foster open communication so that you can address any concerns and celebrate all wins. Setting this meeting up in a structured way creates a regular opportunity for employees to feel that they are being heard. This also gives them the chance to contribute new ideas and stay up to date about any progress that is happening toward company goals, which fosters a sense of inclusion and awareness. Here are some ideas to help you structure your team meetings.

- **Consistency Is Key**: Many in the trades love to cancel meetings or find reasons not to have them, but that's got to change if you are serious about a healthy culture. I find it is best to set a regular schedule by choosing a specific date and time each month. Have attendance be a priority for all team members and let them know that their input is valued.

- **Prepare an Agenda**: Having a simple but structured agenda can keep the meeting focused and more productive. Suggested topics could include:
  » **Company Updates**: This is a time to share any new developments or changes at the company as well as discuss any upcoming projects.
  » **Employee Recognition**: This is a perfect time to acknowledge any employees who went above and beyond in their roles. This can be related to teamwork, excellent customer service, or skill development. It can also be

132

rewarding to acknowledge team members for any personal achievements outside of work.

» **Open Discussion**: This provides the space for employees to bring up any questions, feedback, or concerns they have. It is important to encourage everyone to participate and allow them to share openly.

» **Highlight Wins and Challenges**: Recap any wins from the previous month and discuss any ongoing challenges the team is facing. This is an opportunity to brainstorm solutions together. Your team represents your boots on the ground and can learn and share from one another's experiences.

- **Action Items**: End each meeting by outlining any specific action items from the feedback that was received. Assign responsibilities to the relevant team members and make sure to set deadlines for following up. This way feedback is not just heard but also acted upon.

- **Follow Up and Accountability**: By sending out meeting notes after each session, including any action items and responsibilities, you help maintain accountability and demonstrate that management is taking employee feedback seriously. This continues to build trust over time and allows employees to feel more secure in sharing any feedback.

One-on-One Check-Ins

Consistent one-on-one meetings are essential to establishing trust as well as understanding the needs and goals of each member of your team. These more open conversations create an opportunity for employees to be able to speak freely about their personal progress, as well as any challenges or aspirations they have individually, which will help you understand their areas of strength and where they need help to improve.

These check-ins are relational and are in *addition* to formal reviews. They should focus on the well-being and job satisfaction of the employee. You should ask questions such as, "What has been going well for you lately?" or "Is there anything that you're struggling with right now?" to show genuine interest in what their experiences are like. To do these meetings effectively, here are a few things to keep in mind.

- **No Employee Left Behind**: You should try to schedule these one-on-one meetings twice per year, in addition to a yearly review for each of your employees, and more frequently if company resources allow. Keeping these meetings regular demonstrates your commitment to the growth of your team members and ensures that there will be ongoing communication.

- **Open Dialogue**: Creating a safe space encourages employees to speak openly regarding their experiences, their challenges, and their suggestions. Make sure they know that their thoughts are valued and that they will be kept confidential. Also be sure you are recognizing any of their personal achievements and giving them suggestions that will help with their current obstacles.

- **Forward Focus**: These discussions should focus on goals and improvement. Cover their career goals, opportunities for skill development, and any current progress. Explore their short- and long-term career goals and set actionable steps to support their growth. Ask them for feedback on what is working well at the company and what areas may need improvement.

- **Follow Up**: Show your employees that you are taking their feedback seriously by following up on any issues or goals that were previously discussed. This reinforces accountability and trust—employees see their input is respected. Identify and create any action items for the employee and/or management to continue to support the employee's development.

By nurturing these relationships through one-on-one check-ins, you will create trust and foster an environment where employees feel respected and invested in the success of the company. This not only improves employee morale but also strengthens team bonds and loyalty, which ultimately contributes to a more positive, stickier culture in the workplace.

Bring in the New

We can't leave the subject of sticky culture without acknowledging its role in any new initiatives you're trying to build or any new people who come into the company. I found out the hard way that people hate change and before you can successfully launch new initiatives, it is important to get employees involved in the process. Gathering their ideas, feedback, and suggestions, allows them to help shape the processes and solutions you intend to bring in. This collaborative approach helps employees feel valued and more invested in the success of whatever new initiative you want to introduce. Also, collaborating often leads to even better solutions because employees bring in practical insights from their day-to-day experiences. I refer to this as "filtering the idea before pouring it out on the team."

For example, let's say you'd like to implement a new plan for taking calls after hours. You would write up your ideas and the vision for why you need this at your company. Then, take the following steps.

1. Meet with your management team and ask every question you can think of to pick the idea apart. After that, you can rewrite the idea with any changes needed—making sure all

questions have been addressed. Once that's complete, let some time pass to make sure no other thoughts arise.

2. Once set, call a meeting for team leads (these are your trusted techs who get to brainstorm and beta test things before they go to market). Share the new plan for taking calls after hours, the vision of why it's important, and try to answer all the questions before they're even asked. Once shared, open the floor for criticisms, affirmations, and additional questions. Work through all of those and make any adjustments that make sense.

3. When all the filtering has been done and the managers and team leaders have bought in, then it is time to take it to the techs. Have a meeting with all techs to share the plan, the vision, all the ins and outs, and try to answer all the questions before they are even asked. (This is also a great time to mention that this isn't just *your* new idea. It's something the managers and team leads saw was needed and helped to build as well.)

4. About 99% of the time, you'll find the team loves the idea, there are few questions or clarifications that haven't already been addressed, and everyone can get behind the new plan.

So, before introducing any new initiative, including the ideas from the Leadership Playbook for the Trades, I recommend holding these types of meetings where employees can ask questions, voice concerns, and share ideas. This filtering process helps move new ideas into the company and, by engaging employees in this way, you create a culture of collaboration which garners respect and trust from your team. Employees who feel like their input is valued as these initiatives are being built are much more likely to embrace new strategies as they are rolled out.

And, when your culture is built on valuing your team, you are also more likely to attract new employees. Having quick and flexible onboarding for them helps bring them on—text them, get them in, and give them a quick start date.

If someone new doesn't fit into the culture based on skill set or values, let them go quickly as well. Make it abundantly clear to the team that culture is important for everyone and it requires diligent attention to keep the culture sticky, even if that means doing hard things.

Then, for the employees that you retain, you can set up the kind of healthy compensation and benefit packages that keep them around. Remember, benefits don't have to just be about more money—gym memberships, life insurance, breakfast each morning, jobsite lunches, tickets to local sporting events, and the like can both attract and retain the best employees.

Recap

Creating a sticky culture is about deeply knowing your company's core values and cultivating the kind of environment where your team can feel engaged, valued, and truly aligned with the company's vision. In the trades, we're in the business of service, and customer satisfaction hinges on the morale and performance of your team. Having a strong, sticky company culture is vital to the long-term success of your company. A sticky culture brings in top talent, reduces employee turnover, and encourages team members to take more ownership of their work, which ultimately contributes to more customer satisfaction and higher profitability. That is the highest point for any service company to reach.

Conclusion

WHAT TO DO NEXT

"When someone has been given much, much will be required in return; and when someone has been entrusted with much, even more will be required."
Luke 12:48 (NLT)

I hope after spending time with me in this book, you know how much you have been entrusted with and how important you are in the lives of those you touch with your work. I also hope you can see what an incredible difference it would make to implement the concepts from the Leadership Playbook for the Trades. If you became a healthy owner, cared for and developed your people, laid out your operations with clarity, and got a deeper understanding of your metrics, it would be impossible for you not to move steadily toward your ultimate success.

On this journey together, we've covered a lot:

1. In the first few chapters, we set out to see just how bad things might be for you now. I shared my story and the story of others just like you who made big improvements using the concepts in the Leadership Playbook for the Trades.

   We looked at some common problems you have probably faced or, perhaps, are still facing. Then, you saw ways you can start to deal with those problems in a more productive way based on your results in the assessments.

2. Next, we discussed how all of the important pillars—healthy owner, sticky culture, skilled technicians, efficient operations,

and clear metrics—work together and play off of each other to lead you closer to being able to have a business that can grow sustainably without you burning out.

By the end of that discussion, we demonstrated that the whole framework was built for consistent, incremental improvements to guide you to scale your business with confidence.

3. When we got to Part 2, we started by talking about the pillar of Healthy Owner and how becoming one can have the biggest impact overall by getting you "up the hill" and out of the shit.

We also covered how this key component helps you adjust to find more peace in your business and life.

4. We explored the pillars of Sticky Culture and Skilled Technicians to understand the role of your people in the execution of this vision you are creating, including how to incorporate and support your team members as they grow to do even more.

Once the cultural and skill components for your team were outlined, hopefully you got a greater sense of and appreciation for how those dynamics affect your bottom line.

5. Then, we covered the pillars of Efficient Operations and Clear Metrics to give you a sense of how to set up key pieces of your organization and business so that you can more accurately plan for and track its success.

These pillars can help you foresee coming storms and track how you handled them once they pass.

6. Finally, in Part 3, we applied the playbook to learn some practical steps to start your journey quickly by working through the balance wheel, 5-point alignment assessment, and other questions.

My aim was that the information you discovered through that exploration helps you as you create your vision for yourself and your business and move along your journey of growth.

Throughout it all, I hope you've come to understand the three main points I wanted you to get from this book.

1. You are not a second-class service provider, and you shouldn't be sacrificing your peace to serve your clients.

2. Humility is key and accountability keeps you on track.

3. To effectively scale your business, you need to grow in all five pillars of the Leadership Playbook for the Trades.

If you just start with even two or three clear goals per year, in five short years, you will have accomplished 10 to 15 massive objectives towards creating freedom for yourself and growth for your business. And, if you need help, consider this your call to action...

If you choose to work with us, you will get objective help to guide you in how to communicate, use feedback, make better decisions, and structure your short- and long-term goals. We provide you with support to master your metrics and the loops they create. We want to make sure you're implementing all these processes and systems effectively in a way that supports you and your long-term strategy. We would love to come alongside you, so if you do decide you want help, please reach out to us at hopeforthetrades. com.

I pray that by reading this book you have the found hope and encouragement needed to build your legacy!

Nate Agentis
Hope for the Trades

HOW TO GET MORE HELP

This isn't the leadership step-by-step, checklist, or roadmap; this is the Leadership *Playbook* for the Trades because, just like a playbook in football, it gives you options to run whatever play fits the current situation. Each time you reach a new milestone or a new level in your business, it's good to revisit the playbook with fresh eyes. It is meant to help you reach each next stage of evolution as your company continues to grow into the future.

However, there just wasn't enough room in this book to include over a decade's worth of leadership advice that every owner in the trades needs, so as a thank you from me to you for coming along on the journey to *Get Shit Done*, I am excited to share the following bonus resources with you.

Bonus Material

As mentioned in Chapter 10, you'll find additional tools and information including a template for a one-page strategic plan, a 30-day free trial to SkillCat technician training, tools to help you with hiring technicians, a Special offer to www.Supplyhouse. com's TradeMaster Program, which is a great way to take advantage of exclusive benefits (like free shipping on all orders, free returns, lower pricing on all items, and a dedicated customer service phone line). a template for tracking some of the most important metrics in a trade business, and much more. These bonuses are for you to fill out and develop further. They will help you dig into each of the additional pillars, refine your steps, and see your progress.

Head to www.hopeforthetrades.com/GSDresources for more information.

If you are looking to go deeper still, we have some additional options and resources for your consideration. Sign up for a Hope for the Trades Membership and below you will find many of the benefits you'll receive.

www.hopeforthetrades.com

In-person Teaching

To take this message to a broader audience, you can get more help on topics such as "Preventing Burnout in a Reactive Business," "Healthy Business Culture for the Trades," "Scaling Your Business with Strategic Planning," and more. Nate is ready to bring engaging and inspiring presentations to you and your group or team so that you can encourage growth and learning as your business or organization grows.

www.hopeforthetrades.com/trade-conference-speaker

Technician Training

With our partnership with SkillCat, you can get tailored training solutions for your team. This includes a set of SOPs for the most common HVAC, Plumbing, Electrical and Safety procedures plumbing tasks that every tech should know, a login to a library of training videos to help your technicians master key skills, and a user key for software to track how well your technicians are progressing. Receive a special 30 day free trial.

www.hopeforthetrades.com/technician-training

Learning Curriculum Platform

If you are ready for our highest level of service, you can access our Learning Curriculum Platform that will help you with all the heavy lifting. Get customized training on all 5 pillars of the leadership playbook to help you reach your goals of a healthier life and business and building a lasting legacy. The tailored solutions we provide will help you leave the chaos and burnout behind, unlocking your next level of business potential.

www.hopeforthetrades.com/learning-curriculum

Retreats & Humanitarian Trips

So many people in the trades are burned out and need a respite. Time to reflect, recharge and recapture purpose. We help sponsor and send individuals away to achieve this goal.

There is also a time and place to serve others in need other than on the jobsite. We coordinate and send teams of skills trades people into humanitarian aide sites both domestic and international. **www.hopeforthetrades.com/Humanitarian-aide**

Hope Hub

As a member of Hope for the Trades you will have access to free resources and discounts to key partners that can support your business with Marketing, Material Purchasing, Book Keeping & Accounting, Legal, HR & Payroll, Health Care Benefits, Business Coaching, School Sponsorships and more.

www.hopeforthetrades.com/hopehub

You've come this far, keep moving forward on your journey to find more purpose and peace in your business. Reach out today at **www.instagram.com/hopeforthetrades** for additional information or DM Nate directly at www.instagram.com/hopeforthetrades

ABOUT THE AUTHOR

Nate, a third-generation plumber from Bethlehem, PA, is passionate about improving the lives of individuals, families, and organizations. With over 30 years in plumbing and 15 years of leadership experience, he served as CEO of a multi-million dollar plumbing service company before identifying a gap in the industry and founding Plumbing CEO & Hope for the Trades. Now an author, speaker, and coach, he provides comprehensive technician training and leadership development for plumbing business owners.

Nate's credentials span multiple disciplines, including Plumbing, Management, Marketing, Seminary, and Hague Training. He is committed to organizational health, ethical business practices, and equipping leaders with the tools to scale their trade businesses and drive exponential growth.

For over a decade, Nate has helped individuals and families achieve holistic well-being—mentally, emotionally, and spiritually. He values work-life balance and is dedicated to guiding others toward deeper purpose and fulfillment.

All inquiries for appearances and speaking can be requested at www.hopeforthetrades.com/trade-conference-speaker or you can DM Nate directly at www.instagram.com/hopeforthetrades

www.ingramcontent.com/pod-product-compliance
Lightning Source LLC
Chambersburg PA
CBHW051005140626
46546CB00016B/844